LIVING ALONE
CREATIVELY

Also by Stanley Ely

In Jewish Texas: A Family Memoir

Perfect Mondays

In the Steps of Mister Proust

LIVING ALONE CREATIVELY

CREATIVELY

✦

HOW TWELVE PEOPLE DO IT

Stanley E. Ely

iUniverse, Inc.

New York Lincoln Shanghai

LIVING ALONE CREATIVELY
HOW TWELVE PEOPLE DO IT

iUniverse books may be ordered through booksellers or by contacting:

iUniverse
2021 Pine Lake Road, Suite 100
Lincoln, NE 68512
www.iuniverse.com
1-800-Authors (1-800-288-4677)

ISBN-13: 978-0-595-38761-8 (pbk)
ISBN-13: 978-0-595-83143-2 (ebk)
ISBN-10: 0-595-38761-6 (pbk)
ISBN-10: 0-595-83143-5 (ebk)

Printed in the United States of America

For Felice, Janet A., Tom, Shelley, Glenn, Nancy, Greg,
Susan, Wayne, Janet B., and Jodi,
the people who opened their hearts
and generously shared their stories for this book.

"I love to be alone. I never found the companion that was so companion-able as solitude. We are for the most part more lonely when we go abroad among men than when we stay in our chambers."

—Henry David Thoreau, *Walden; or, Life in the Woods*

Contents

Acknowledgments

Friends shared with me many excellent suggestions in the writing of this book.

To them go my sincere thanks:

Margie Barab, Jeanette Doronzo, Elissa Ely, Murray Friedman, Arch Garland, Phyllis Goldman, David Groff, Charles Salzberg, Matt Sartwell, Julie Schieffelin, and Doris Shapiro.

S.E.E.

Introduction

How many mothers have you met who sent a child into the world hoping he or she would end up living alone? None, did you say?

And how many of those sons or daughters grew up with the intention to live alone? Probably not many more.

Yet, consider these numbers:

…The year 2000 census counts eighty-six million single adults living in this country—more than ever before.

…Twelve percent of American women and sixteen percent of men now enter their forties never having wed, the highest percentage in the nation's history.

…Women now actually spend more of their adult lives single than married.

…In 2003 nearly twenty-seven percent of American households consisted of one person living alone.

Potent statistics, aren't they?

Some of those singles are in a relationship with another person. And it's a safe bet that others are looking for one. But not all.

There are plenty of people who are dedicated to living a life that is rich and full without a companion or spouse. They have reached their mature years unsubscribed to the belief that a complete life dictates settling in with a mate. In this book you will meet twelve of them.

Though searching for a partner may not have been wiped from their screens, they are not postponing a satisfying life until—if—that partner is found.

How did they reach this point? It wasn't by following a quick 1-2-3-step program toward single happiness but by facing struggles and challenges and incorporating creative components to living their lives alone. Besides Henry David Thoreau, the famous loner, the list of artists who were unpartnered is long: Emily Dickinson, Marcel Proust, Vincent van Gogh, Edouard Vuillard, Federico García Lorca, Eudora Welty, and scores of others.

These artists were endowed with genius. But the creative component referred to here doesn't imply a gift for painting or writing or composing. "Creative" here means facing circumstances with activities and attitudes that are imaginative, rejuvenating, challenging, and that sometimes mean standing up to usual convention.

Other books have explored the single life but not focused on introducing people who make being single a successful, ongoing lifestyle. This book does that.

◆   ◆   ◆

Being a person who has tried to make a good life for himself alone, at least most of the time, I'll include myself at the end of the book. But before introducing others and myself, I'll offer an opinion: It's that the world seems to be mostly populated by two kinds of people—the marrying and the non-marrying kind. (This excludes past generations when there was heavy pressure for everyone to get married and they did, happily or not.) Haven't we all known a man or a woman who breaks up with (or maybe loses) a partner, only before the calendar can move to a new month hears a knock at the door from the next suitor, hair combed, bouquet in hand? And this without even doing a search?

The other camp is populated with people who don't ever seem to locate the right boyfriend, girlfriend, husband, or wife. Maybe an affair gets underway, but mostly it's based on sex, and when the window shade goes up in the morning or a few mornings later, the companion looks disappointingly less interesting—Perhaps even boring. And this scenario is repeated until the man or woman faces up not to the unavailability of Mister or Miss Right but to the maybe reluctant admission that Mister or Miss Right may not be the desired object. At such a point, our unmarried man or woman either despairs of that state or determines just to muddle through.

There is a third camp, and that is those people who come out of a relationship or marriage to discover that they prefer to build a fulfilling life alone rather than to look for a new partner, that they find maybe unexpected virtue in being unpartnered. You'll meet some of those people in this book.

To determine making a good life alone seems to require that being married or partnered not be viewed as categorically preferable. Envy of the person wearing a wedding ring needs to stop if it ever started (as it has done for me). Society doesn't help in that regard. A character in Thornton Wilder's play *Our Town* remarks that most folks go to the grave two by two.

If you are one who is single, you'll manage better by stamping "OK" on yourself as single. That means granting yourself permission to attend a movie alone, to go out to dinner alone (which may be harder for women than men), to put on a nice outfit and show up at a party alone, even if most other guests arrive in pairs, and, finally, to put on your coat and head home, satisfied with the evening.

Those goals may be harder to reach than they sound. There certainly have been times when I didn't like attending a party alone and when I wasn't happy going home alone. Thus, you've got to create one more stamp that says, "Don't expect perfection." Sometimes being alone can mean being alone when alone is what you don't want to be. Lonely times are lonely times, and regrets have to be allowed. As one of the singles in this book says, "Yes, I feel sad sometimes, and that's OK. I wish I felt it less often, and that's OK, too."

I'd say that the single person confronts other challenges as well. If you're past a certain age, you face the platoon of friends and acquaintances who wonder, as they surely do, why an eligible man or woman like you is alone. You might have psychological insights to offer an explanation, but the world doesn't care about that. They just see your single name on the door. That's when it's time to stand tall and look and feel—-and maybe even say—that life is agreeable as it is.

◆　　　◆　　　◆

Many couples consciously work to reach a successful relationship. In the same way, there are individuals who are single and strive to achieve a fulfilling life without the closeness of another person, knowing that it doesn't just drop in their laps. This holds true whether their single status is brief or long.

The men and women you will meet in this book are people of this sort. They represent an array of professions, ages, lifestyles, religions, and geographical locales. Some are coming out of marriages or past lovers, some have never been married or had long-term partners. A few have had children or have adopted children. *None* has waited for a gratifying life to arrive at their door; all have worked for it. Satisfaction, not perfection, has been their goal. And all have been extraordinarily candid about sharing their past and present lives with us.

In getting to know them, I've learned that, despite their different histories, the people in this book share some common traits.

…Several people in the book say they believe they were always meant to live alone, although for years they did not do so. "Maybe," one concludes, "many of us don't want to live alone even when we know we should."

…Some believe that their happiest moments are those spent volunteering or teaching, and several realized that in sacrificing or attending to the needs of others, they neglected to attend to their own and are setting out to correct that now.

…Several found that they prefer to live alone and that it came as a surprising discovery after years of being in a relationship.

....Many say that they rarely experience loneliness not only because of a busy life but also from a developed ability to work or play or amuse themselves by themselves.

...And, it seems that the idealized concept of happiness is not what these people hold as an objective. "I don't expect my days to be pure happiness," says one. "In fact, happiness is not a goal."

These traits are explored fully in the chapters that follow, each of which begins with one or two significant facets of the person's life that a reader can emulate.

◆   ◆   ◆

In reading this book, don't expect to hit upon a formula that will suddenly eliminate sadness or loneliness or even ambivalence. Anyone who says that none of those conditions exist in their lives is certainly cutting into the truth. They seem inescapable in every human's life, as much for those profiled here as for anyone else.

Some of the people in this book possess true artistic ability that informs their creative lives—ability not shared by many. But others, not born with that talent and while not holding out for eternal joy, have found and developed fulfilling components in their lives that help ward off those moments of sadness or loneliness. What they *all* have in common is a willingness to embrace challenges and risk change and also to know that accepting realistic compromise is not a cowardly way of simply backing off.

This book is not written to advocate an unpartnered lifestyle. If, however, you are living without a partner and seek a deeper degree of fulfillment, I hope that someone or something you read about here will offer help in that direction. That is its purpose.

Gardening and Journal Keeping: Felice Picano

"Since there's nobody like that in my life today, I tell the journal what I tell nobody else," says Felice Picano, referring to his lover, who died of AIDS in 1991. "I use the journal now in a way that I didn't when my partner was alive. But long before that, all along actually, it allowed me to kvetch and share information and where it turns out to also lie to myself, as I did at times."

Felice may find journal keeping especially valuable today, but it has been a part of his life all the years since 1968 when, at age twenty-four, he undertook the custom as part of daily life. He is far from alone in the habit. Journal keeping remains an honored tradition, available to anyone with pencil and paper and a few quiet moments alone. Some people without a partner have found the journal to become one.

In the case of Felice, a successful, well-published writer, the creative drive that produced and continues to produce a stream of books and scripts has been nourished by his volumes of journals. "They have helped transform me from an ordinary person into a writer," he believes. They also form a historical marker in portraying East Coast gay life over several decades, including that of the 1970s, a time filled with partying, sex, and drugs, the specter of AIDS not yet known. (The journals and papers that cover his years 1968 to 1990 are now in the Beinicke Library at Yale University.)

Felice credits his journal partner with something more—repaying the debt by helping shape him, the writer. In a 1998 interview in the *New York Blade News*, Felice is quoted as saying of *The Lure*, his novel published in 1977, twenty years earlier, "I don't even know who the author of that book is any more. I'm not him either as a writer or a person." The change effected in him by his own writing is something he consciously planned and set out to do years ago, he believes.

"In the '60s," he says, "I was part of a group that thought you could alter yourself by what you did and how you did it as well as how you mentally nurtured yourself. I called my journals 'The Diary of an Alchemist' because I really wanted to become the golden ideal of what alchemy is about." Along with meditation and yoga, writing, he says, has been one of the methods he has used to become a different person. "Of course, AIDS and gay and world politics have changed my life, too. Who was I? A middle-class boy from a middle-class family in Queens, New York City, and I turned into an artist."

◆   ◆   ◆

Without his long-time partner and what Felice describes as "an enormous number" of other friends, he packed up and moved from New York to Los Angeles in 1995. Even with a sprinkling of West Coast acquaintances and an established reputation as a writer, Felice faced a future alone on the opposite side of the country from where he had always lived. It happened at a point in life when most others are contentedly digging in to stay put in familiar surroundings.

Felice seems renewed by California outdoor life and what it has sown in him: a passion for hiking, climbing, studying plants and flowers, cultivating vegetables, and cooking. With a head of snow-white hair and a white goatee, tanned complexion, polo shirt, and perennial shorts, he could pass today for a native. So complete is his California transformation that except for book promotion he largely avoids trips back to New York. "I get sick every time I go there," he says.

An East Coast friend takes umbrage. "Don't you miss the subways? Doing anything in Los Angeles always seems so difficult. Driving half an hour to go not very far. Don't you miss the place where you lived for fifty years!"

Apparently not. Felice owns an unflashy, decade-old car that gets him around when he needs to get around, a car known to have provided him transportation as far north as San Francisco and even Vancouver. But for him, the wheels haven't become the indispensable companion they are for many Californians. He works long hours and has days when he doesn't leave his house. Solitary activities—writing, gardening—-that others might find isolating, Felice seems to find nourishing. "I could be busy every night of the week if I wanted to," he says. "But I don't." Even cooking for one and experimenting with recipes he seems to find pleasurable, a creative distraction.

Felice's interests in hiking and gardening have been helped along by the difference between his living accommodations in New York and California. The West Village loft he occupied in Manhattan enjoyed a view no farther than a tiny space across a narrow street and a narrow slice of the Hudson River to the west. It has been replaced by a nearly mountain-high aerie with a panoramic vista over a good chunk of Los Angeles, plus, if the atmosphere allows, a view as far as the Pacific Ocean. Pitched on the edge of a hill, his address is the unpretentious two-story, glassed-in guest quarters of a larger house, found on a curving, steep climb that ascends from the West Hollywood part of Sunset Boulevard.

New York has masses of people, Los Angeles masses of cars, but Felice's abode avoids both. His days at home often translate into not seeing another human being, which seems to bother him not at all. Surrounded mostly by sky, his house is usually warm by day, always cool by night. All that interrupts the surrounding silence is an occasional dog barking from a house down the hill.

With windows all around, the sun beams into his home so brightly that he has to pull the shades in his downstairs work area in the afternoon. That room, both office, library, and bedroom, overflows with photos and shelves crammed with hundreds of books.

With terraces outside, plus spacious, fertile beds all along the side, Felice's domain is an ideal place for planting lettuce, tomatoes, broccoli, cauliflower, cabbage, parsley, potatoes, onions, leeks, eggplant, and beets, each of which he has learned to successfully cultivate. While his parents grew flowers and fruit in a large yard in Queens, raising vegetables has become a new experience for their son. He knows now to rotate them around to find where they will thrive, and he experiments with tasty ways of combining them in cooking.

Eager to share in the home-grown crop and Felice's talent in the kitchen, a New York friend planning to arrive at the start of April says, "Push the veggies to come up early this year, so we can have something from the garden."

"Veggies come up here *all* year," replies the writer with a huff. This seems to be true, since, though barely into spring, dinner prepared for the friend's visit included soup and salad invented with a variety of vegetables no more than half a day from the garden just outside the door.

After the fresh-from-the-ground dinner, the East Coast visitor is guided on a trip to the Getty Center that dominates the landscape above Brentwood, near the ocean. The tour includes a stroll around the Getty's imposing circular gardens that seem as familiar to Felice as his own at home. "Plants get changed here regularly, four times a year," he comments, as the two inhale the passing scent of orange blossoms and continue on by yellow mimosa and jacaranda trees and the multitude of other plants of vibrant colors. Felice is able to identify each plant, along with its ideal growing conditions.

The New Yorker's acquaintance with plants being limited to a few leafy specimens that struggle for survival in a shady apartment, he follows humbly as his transplanted friend lectures on the difference between a daisy and its look-alike cousin, the euryops. "Do you know the replacement plants as well as these?" hesitates the New Yorker. A silent nod gives the answer.

◆   ◆   ◆

In spite of what Easterners may think, Southern California is no creative wasteland, according to Felice. The fear that his friends had, that he would have no one to talk to and that he would never write another word, has not materialized. Having published thirteen books over twenty years before switching coasts, Felice has brought out another six books since then plus a produced play and three movie scripts. He has been a featured speaker at numerous writing conferences in the U.S. and Canada and has served as a judge for several writing awards.

"I came out to California constantly before deciding I really wanted to move here, you know," Felice says. "Those trips convinced me that there was a good chance of developing an interesting life, aside from enjoying the natural beauty. The real clue occurred on my last trip, a year before I moved. I'd come to Los Angeles in the winter for a two-week stay, and I found excuses to keep extending it to finally six weeks. When I did fly back to New York, I forgot half the clothing I'd brought at a friend's house. You don't have to be Freud to figure out what I was feeling."

His new locale is invigorating culturally in ways that the East Coast isn't. "People in different arts mingle much more in California--Los Angeles *and* San Francisco—than in New York, where writers tend to stick with writers, and so on. As for work, one can sit at a computer and send e-mail here as well as in New York."

There were somber factors that precipitated Felice's need for a change of scene. Though in his New York youth he learned as much Yiddish as his neighborhood Jewish pals, Felice's family there is almost all deceased and his past, he says, "has become increasingly meaningless." "Plus," he stresses, "I had no friends left in New York. They all died of AIDS."

Though that may be an exaggeration, those deaths did include four from the Violet Quill, a group of then-young gay writers who met for a couple of years in the early 1980s to read to each other from their works in progress. Several of them became the most important gay authors of the decade. Of the original seven, only Felice and two others, Andrew Holleran and Edmund White, survive.

Felice's partner, Bob Lowe, also died from AIDS in 1991. They met on the set of the documentary film *Pumping Iron* in 1975, and although for the most part the two men did not share an apartment, their time together lasted sixteen years. Felice says that California is brighter than anywhere else he knows of, and moving there helped him put the lights back on after Bob's death. Thirteen years later, Felice has come to re-examine their relationship. "What I think now is either how selfish Bob was or what bad timing he had, by being so great while he was alive that few could ever compete, then dying when he did, leaving me at my half-century mark, when, let's face it, my chance of ever meeting anyone as terrific had dropped so low."

There were others who also were lost to AIDS. Vito Russo, the well-regarded writer and film maker of *The Celluloid Closet*, was one. "Vito always greeted me with, 'Hiya, sweeties,' but to most people he was prickly and fast to take offense," Felice recalls. "His last days in the hospital were very different, so serene." David Feinberg, a writer, was another. "David kept phoning me a week before his death to plot a trip to Los Angeles for Carrie Fisher's birthday party. I don't know how much he believed he'd be able to accomplish, dragging IV tubes up an airplane aisle."

The loss of these promising figures in the arts created an irreplaceable vacuum in New York's cultural community in the late 1980s and early '90s, and in Felice's own life. "I nursed so many through the end stages of a terrible disease," he says, some of those memories still fresh and hurtful well more than a decade later. "It's hard for anyone who wasn't involved in the epidemic at that time to appreciate the impact of those men's deaths."

◆   ◆   ◆

While crowds of single people may try to flee an unpartnered life for one with another person, there are others who travel the opposite direction. Felice is one such person. Despite the years with his partner in New York, he says, "I believe I was always a person who was going to live alone. I happened to hook up with a guy who was the marrying kind, and as long as Bob was alive, I was married to him. Even within that marriage, however, he made big spaces for me. I really think that wanting to live alone is who I was all along."

Some people can look back to the origins of this kind of feeling. In Felice's case, it stems from being a middle child, with both older and younger siblings, but enough years apart from him that he remembers the feeling of growing up on his own. "My siblings were off doing things, and I got used to it and never considered it a problem. I still have an image of myself at age six and seven, spread out on the floor in sunlight, writing and coloring in notebooks. I think I learned to amuse myself pretty early."

Even so, he points out that one can go through phases, as he himself did. "When I was a teenager and even a young adult, I was very social, living with family or roommates. Those were the years when one really wanted to be part of a group. But once I was no longer with others…well, I didn't really miss them. Wanting that connection to a crowd as a young person, while in college, might grow into a wish for partnering later…and still later, maybe a wish not to."

By his own admission, Felice's tendency toward a solitary life seems surprising since he clearly has a social side with a wide circle of friends, fifty of whom attended his sixtieth birthday party early in 2004. A proud part of his furnishings at home are paintings done by friends and gifts handmade for him. But his social life doesn't compete with the quiet home on the hill. "I have people here who pressure me to look for a new partner," he says. "Mostly they're paired off themselves. I wonder sometimes if all the hassling from these people is because misery loves company. I ask whether they have any good candidates, but they don't. In any case I'm too busy living and working. I don't see where or how I'd fit another person into my life now."

Like many seniors, and perhaps especially for those who live alone, issues of health take on increased importance for Felice. With no employer-provided health insurance and concerned with his long-standing high blood pressure, in 2003 he enrolled in a study at a nearby clinic that monitors his physical condition on a monthly basis. Aside from the benefit that will accrue to himself, he points out that these studies help the government decide how best to use various medicines still undergoing testing.

Recently, Felice had what he considers an important test of his solitary lifestyle when he faced a significant health problem. Although during the previous year he had hiked 10,200 feet up at Yosemite Park, it was in his own steep driveway that one day he suddenly slid and badly sprained his foot and ankle in several places. A real trial for one who lives alone ensued. The healing would take over two months, the beginning of which occurred during the year-end holidays of 2004 when he would normally travel to visit friends in Santa Barbara and Palm Springs. With painkillers daily, long drives were out of the question, and with a swollen foot and in need of a cane, crowded events needed to be cancelled, too. To that was added a rainy winter, which kept him housebound.

The timing of the accident wasn't altogether bad. A week earlier, Felice had decided to turn one of his novels into a screenplay, and he had just laid out his plans. During the first month of invalidism, he concentrated on that project, and there were dozens of books needing to be read for judging a literary award, too. The author had more work than he knew what to do with.

"A few close friends drove me longer distances, and short trips I could handle myself," he says. At a dinner party he gave later, one pal who has been coupled for years asked who had cared for him during the difficult period. "Who do you think?" Felice answered. "My three staunchest buddies…me, myself, and I." He says that he never once felt deprived and thinks that he and his life choice passed the crisis without ever flirting with the supposed pangs of loneliness.

◆   ◆   ◆

In being without a partner, Felice places himself as part of an increasing trend in our society. "In the twenty-first century more young people are choosing to live alone," he notes, "and they may be in the vanguard of what human society is going to look like in the twenty-second." Perhaps, he says, the tendency for young people to spend so much time in front of a computer will meld into their remaining single later on. Certainly, he hears of parents who are sending their children to summer camp just to move them outside with other kids and away from a computer screen.

But a balance has to be struck, that between time alone and time spent with others. "It's extremely rare, but when I don't want to be by myself, I phone or e-mail someone," says Felice. "We go hiking or to the theater, or to the new Disney Music Hall. Los Angeles is a more interesting place than it once was." That theater or outdoor companion is as likely to be someone younger as well as someone his own age. "Those young people who are living alone also require company. Sometimes it's semi-parental company. Last year I got two Father's Day cards!" (Trebor Healey, a much younger friend, observes, "Felice doesn't need a partner to be loving as he's such a good friend to so many.")

In Felice's view, it is seniors who find the most difficulty in striking a satisfactory balance between enjoying solitude and seeking company. "I watch what happens to older people as their friends and loved ones die and they are left alone. In the grocery store, for instance, I see older people finding reasons to delay leaving, inventing any excuse to keep the clerk at the checkout counter engaged in conversation. It's sad. They just don't have anyone else to talk to."

As for himself, he has the constant stream of new work, reaching increasingly beyond traditional books to film and theater. And the birds who come around every morning for breakfast keep him company. "Now I know who they are," says Felice. "There's a pair of mockingbirds who have built a nest and they do a good job of defending it so other flying creatures don't muscle in. These birds not only are beautiful, they make it easier for me to grow vegetables because they keep down a lot of the insect population."

Then there are the plants in his garden that call for feeding, watering, and sometimes rearranging. Felice says that there is less distance and more of a connection between gardening and writing than one might think. "In gardening, you plant something in the ground and watch it blossom into something big, and it's then harvested and used by somebody to nurture them. That's true for books and stories and plays, too. It's just that one is done mentally and the other physically. It has taken me three or four years to write some books, so I sure have the patience to wait a season for something to grow out of the ground."

Felice also profits from the sunny bedroom and expansive view from a balcony just outside the glass front wall of his home. When he needs it, he can enjoy the companionship of interesting, talented people, including a regular flow of friends who visit from out of town.

It strikes the visitor that Felice is by himself only insofar as romantic partnerships are concerned. In his adopted California lifestyle, he has intimacy with the abundance of nature at his door—plants, flowers, birds, and sun—and the good that it has done for him gives him no reason to want to return back East.

In any case, he says, "Living alone is what's happening, and here I am living in the now. If that somehow changes, maybe I'll change too. I have my journal so I guess I won't end up walking around the streets talking to myself or dragging out a conversation with a grocery clerk. I figure it's up to me to amuse myself a life."

◆   ◆   ◆

Trebor Healey, a young gay writer whom Felice has guided and encouraged and who won a fiction award for a first novel in 2004, says: "Felice is that rare writer who is always available to lend a hand to up-and-coming writers. He's also a fabulous cook and he always seems to share the huge crop from his garden, a telling symbol of his nurturing ways."

Discovering Yoga:
Janet Aschkenasy

Yoga classes abound in this country today. Some people practice it purely for the physical gain, some for the spiritual/health benefit, many for a combination of the two. For Janet Aschkenasy, a single New Yorker in her early forties, it seems that yoga was the door that, once opened in the late 1990s, brought her to clarity and strength and allowed her to accept dark moments. Though she continues her work at home as a freelance business writer, yoga, she says, both practicing and teaching, has transformed her life. "Teaching it," Janet says, "is hands-down my favorite thing to do."

All that that happened practically by accident, although Janet has no strong belief in accidents. "My maternal grandmother was my closest friend," she says, "and a lot of obligations started falling into my lap in the months leading to her dying. I had to take over household and business responsibilities while at the same time running a magazine that was a bare-boned operation. I was a bundle of tension, trying to do so many things at once, including commuting from Manhattan to Long Island. It reached the point where I went to one of the managers at my magazine and said that I needed to take some time off.

"His answer was remarkable. 'Janet,' he said, 'you have to do something more than a vacation, something life-changing.' And he suggested that I check out a new-age spa in the Catskills in upstate New York." Janet followed his advice and went to the spa. Though the trip was not for yoga, while there—it was in 1999, when her grandmother was still living—-she started to take what she called the "house" (basic) yoga classes. She returned to the spa a few more times following that first visit, one of them on a cold Christmas weekend. "That was a lonely, sad time for me," Janet recalls. "I sort of unenthusiastically went back to a yoga class, and what happened in that class was an immense surprise: I found that moving and breathing in a particular way could open up a new channel in me. It was the last thing I expected, a joyful experience.

"When the class ended, I went up and told the teacher about what had happened. He said that I needed to continue with yoga at home, and he referred me to a teacher in Manhattan. I began to practice yoga here, and within five years I was teaching twice a week in the same studio where I went as a student, plus teaching as a volunteer at a public health clinic in Manhattan."

According to Janet, yoga offers life changes, and it has done so for her. Speaking from solid experience, she says, "The really brilliant part of yoga is that when you practice consistently, the part of the mind that you use all the time is able to quiet down and your inner intelligence begins to speak to you and guides you where you should go."

Even well involved in the practice of yoga, Janet still, at times, feels disconnected from everything and somewhat lost. Then, she says, she asks for guidance and direction. Those are the occasions when she's apt just to sit quietly in front of a candle. "But I don't wait for those moments to get in touch with myself. I do it every morning when I'm practicing, opening and breathing, slowing myself down. There is a mind that's very useful, but if I can step away from it for awhile and just look at it, that for me is the doorway to freedom and awareness."

◆   ◆   ◆

Before teaching yoga, Janet had the idea of writing about it, particularly about incorporating sound into the exercises. And she has done so. In an article called "Sound Healing" in a 2003 issue of *Spirituality and Health*, she writes, as the subtitle says, about "the ancient art and new science of using sounds and voices to treat pain and life-threatening disease." She tells of women who used "humming and toning (creating sound with an elongated vowel for an extended period), together with the chanting of Sanskrit verse and seed syllables, to ease the pain of childbirth."

The combination, Janet writes, "deepens the breath while often creating a hypnotic sea of vocals that can foster profound relaxation and may deeply affect even extreme pain." Such sounds, Janet goes on, "can help cancer victims withstand the rigors of chemotherapy and even go on living lives they'd been told were finished."

These are techniques that Janet employs in the classes she teaches. "There is no guarantee that sound-based healing will work miracles for everyone," she says. "And it's also important to understand that 'healing' is not exclusively about relieving pain—sometimes quite the contrary. People frequently need ways to sit with pain, to learn its lessons and literally become friends with what ails them. Tools like sound and yoga can guide us in that process—even if it means accepting that a cancer will not, in fact, be cured."

"Still," she adds, "even the simplest humming exercise can be an effective stress or headache reliever."

Janet's students have reported that they sleep better after a class that incorporated sounds and voices. A woman whose history includes having been "discarded" as an infant in a bathroom said that she felt "at home" during the yoga class. One HIV-positive student had a significant increase in his vital T-cell count after several months of consistent classes.

Janet sends out a loud cautionary note, however. "Telling these kinds of stories make people think there's something wrong if they *don't* have the same experience as others have had. Individuals have their own processes of healing and resolution. Your path may be very different from that of the person on the next mat."

People do seek different results and have different experiences with yoga. Says Janet, "If someone comes just for the physical exercise, that's fine, but for me, without the emphasis on breathing, yoga becomes mostly calisthenics. There is not a lot of variation in the poses I teach, and my objective is not to give a series of progressively more difficult exercises. I aim for relaxation and awareness of the internal experience."

Those are the pleasures of teaching yoga, of sharing with others what the teacher has gained. But there are challenges, especially when the teacher works with students who are seriously ill.

"I'm thinking of a woman who has had the worst kind of cancer and keeps getting the worst kind of diagnoses," Janet says. "There's a kind of squeamishness that many people would have coming into contact with that. It's something you might well not want to see, or to handle by saying 'poor you.' But there can also be a certain maturity, a certain godliness where you can look at that person eye-to-eye with all their infirmity and trouble and just…be there. You're not fawning over them, you're not pulling back, you're just in the space with them. As a yoga teacher, that's what I want to have, *have* to have. That's a real mode of healing."

Just before Thanksgiving 2004, the happy relationship Janet had with a Manhattan yoga studio abruptly ended when her teacher, who had run the studio for a dozen years, called to say that it was not making money and that he was going to close it. "I was shocked," Janet says. "Our studio had served as a unique place of healing, and I felt truly at home there as a teacher. Its inherent kindness—its commitment to slowness, breath, and the inner experience—was an antidote to the 'no pain, no gain' mentality we Americans are so in love with. The place had its own problems, but you actually felt the walls singing with something else."

Though angered at being thrust out of the nest in that way, Janet says she knew that's exactly what it was—time to leave the nest. "We closed the studio the third week of December. I tried to live my teaching, to let my emotions be present, to sit with pain, to feel the loss and to feel lost, and for two weeks I cried a hell of a lot. I knew I'd be teaching elsewhere, though, and I'd already set things in motion at a spiritual center a few blocks from where I live, where I had given some workshops. When I got the news, I found another spot where I could rent space and teach an extra weekly class. Months before, I'd begun practicing yoga at a different venue too, since my own cherished teacher was on sabbatical and I could no longer study with him in New York. I remember him quoting his own teacher as to how the stones serve to massage the river."

According to Janet, there is a rhythm and intelligence to all that has transpired, including the need to abandon a place of protection and nurturing and discover the inner oasis yet again. "I think I was ripe for this latest rebirth," she concludes. "And yes, there is a connection with Grandma, because that kind of acceptance is what she gave to me."

◆   ◆   ◆

It was one of those dreadful days at age six or seven when you've been teased by older kids going home on the school bus, the hurt so stinging that you rush inside fighting to hold back tears, determined never to go back to school. The villains who did the teasing don't seem to lodge those events in their memories; the ones teased do.

When it happened to Janet, she ran for comfort to her grandparents' house, where she was living with them and her mother. "My grandmother had an idea," says Janet so wistfully that remembering it decades later—envisioning even what the bus looked like—brings on something between a smile and a tear. "We'll make a mask," her grandmother stated.

"A mask?"

"Yes, a scary mask that you can wear tomorrow on the bus."

Without a better plan, Janet dried her tears and scooted up to the table with the elder lady. The two of them began to work with construction paper and paste, paint, and string. By dinnertime they had created an ugly devil with horrible teeth and eyes. Janet strapped it on hesitantly as she boarded the bus the next morning. Still frightened, something now told her she could manage. If her bigger classmates had been planning further torture, there was no sign of it. When the bus arrived at school, the mask came off.

The mask has stayed off. At age forty-three, Janet Aschkenasy is a tall, slender lady of clear skin and deep-set eyes and a voice that sounds (and is) like that of a singer. The nervousness she reveals with a new acquaintance changes quickly into a manner comfortable, open, and very forthright once calmly seated in her apartment. Never married, Janet lives by herself in a Manhattan co-op, dividing a full schedule between freelance writing and her commitment to the practice and teaching of yoga. Calling herself mostly vegetarian, she radiates the good health that she works to pass on to her students. But much of the strength and good that she is today she attributes to the lasting love and influence of her grandmother, which lasted for decades, even past the grandmother's death at eighty-seven in the year 2000.

The closeness of Janet and her mother's mother, whom she always called Grandma, began when Janet was around age two. Her parents, in Janet's words, had had a short-lived marriage, and she and her mother moved in with her mother's parents on Long Island. Both of her grandparents were educated people. "He was a dentist who for years worked out of an office in their house, she had been a music major at Hunter College in Manhattan. Many were the nights when I would sit at Grandma's side at the piano, turning the pages as she and I got through favorites from *The Sound of Music.*. She loved to play and didn't even mind trying her hand at some of my favorite rock songs. Actually, whatever I wanted to do—creatively—found my grandmother's enthusiasm. With her it felt safe to try out anything."

Janet says that everyone in her family was into art and music in one way or another. Her mother had been a talented artist, and there were canvases plus finished paintings everywhere in their house, an artist's studio in the attic. "You don't have to be a great artist to do watercolors. I started doing them when I was in junior-high school, and I've kept it as a hobby," she says, pointing out one design she has incorporated on her business card and several others that hang in her apartment. The singing lessons she began at around age twelve also set her on a future path, which she continues to use in teaching the form of yoga that employs chant and other vocables to lengthen and deepen breath.

But it was Janet's grandmother whose influence reigned above the rest and whose passing struck as her greatest loss. "My grandmother was tall and dark-haired with an understated elegance about her all of her life," Janet recalls. "She enjoyed wearing good clothing, but she wasn't flashy like many of the women in our suburban neighborhood. My grandfather was immersed in his dental practice, and my grandmother held the purse strings, ran the house, and supervised everyone and everything in it. She was the complete head of family, the one who kept the books and handled the investments and made sure things and people and schedules were taken care of. She was generous and sharp minded and used to being in control. She longed to travel but felt it was her place to stay by her husband who was more of a homebody. At her funeral, the most accurate and touching thing the rabbi said about my grandmother was, 'There was a queenliness about her.'

"For most people, it is their mother who is their rock, their support, the person they always know will be there. For me, it was my grandmother, and when she disappeared from my life five years ago, I had an experience that most people would describe as falling apart. But falling apart can turn into a way of coming into yourself, finding your strength and who you are, and I'm still in that process…big time!

"Behind all the singing and piano playing was my grandmother's acceptance of whatever I did. Nurturing, caring, and loving—you can bring those traits forth for people who aren't your children or any relation. These are qualities I try to cultivate as a yoga teacher. It's a great way to keep my grandmother's legacy alive."

◆   ◆   ◆

Before there was yoga in Janet's life, there was journalism, and though she has lived away from her father most of her life, she remains in contact with him and credits him with first noticing her flair for writing and encouraging it as a profession. "I was an English major at the State University of New York at Albany," she says, "and my dad wanted me to come out of college not just with a degree but with having done an internship that would give me some writing clips to show." In her senior year she interned at the state legislature in Albany. It fit her father's plan since part of the intern's job was to produce a newspaper out of the weekly legislative committee meetings. The interns, unpaid, did the writing and even delivered the papers to the offices of the legislators.

"I was randomly assigned to—yikes—the banking committee," recalls Janet. "Me, who had never done anything with finance. To be pushed out into the legislature and meet important people was really scary when you're twenty-one and have never interviewed anybody. But it was an incredible experience to move through that fear and learn that you can make a story if you know how to ask questions and keep an inquisitive mind. It was in the internship where I realized that I enjoyed gleaning information from actual people rather than from books or research reports. By the time I graduated in 1983, I had a book of press clippings about banking.

"I stepped forward and called myself a financial writer. Through an article I saw in *The New York Times*, I landed a job with an insurance trade book. The thing is, there were very few women in the insurance business in those days. Later, I heard one of my editors say, 'Well, we didn't think it would hurt to have a woman.' They felt a female reporter would stand out in a crowd."

From there, Janet went on to be insurance editor at *The Journal of Commerce*, then to *Reuters*, and in the mid-1990s she made a connection to a monthly magazine written for people in the pensions and employee benefits business. She became their managing editor and reaped glowing reviews. All the same, she lost her job in a downsizing phase three-and-a-half years after starting at the magazine. "It was another scary moment," she says, "but it made me realize that I didn't want to go back and do the nine-to-five thing with a publishing organization. I had already freelanced so I knew I could do that if need be."

Today Janet is once again a freelance writer, contributing to both her former magazine and other finance publications. Though she has increasingly become a devotee of yoga, it is that freelance work, the culmination of twenty years experience as a journalist first encouraged by her father, that pays most of her bills and, she says, is a creative way to earn a living.

◆   ◆   ◆

"All my life I've believed in God," Janet says, "and my grandmother used to say, 'You're not alone, honey, God is with you,' but recently I've come closer to understanding that in a way that's really meaningful to me. I feel that there's a benevolent presence within me, always."

She keeps that presence alive while continuing to write, practice and teach yoga, and spend time with her family, which still plays a front-row part in her life. Her family includes a half-sister from her father's second marriage and her mother. "My mother met my dad on a trip to Israel, and when she came back, she did amazing paintings from memory of the Israeli landscape and the children. She depicted on canvas what we Jews often sing about in Hebrew: a land of milk and honey. But after her divorce, Mom was never quite the same and never fully resumed her art work."

Now, with her Grandma gone, Janet spends a lot of time caring for her mother. It has caused her to focus on elder care, a topic that she wrote about in *Financial Planning* magazine in 2005. She reported that on a five-point scale where five is very stressful, many caregivers of older people said that taking care of the person they help rates a four or five. Finding time for themselves, and balancing work and family responsibilities ranked as the most frequently unmet needs of those caregivers.

To apply this knowledge to herself, Janet has begun to attend a support group of daughters and sons of mentally ill parents sponsored by the National Association for Mental Illness. Added to that was a weeklong yoga retreat in Costa Rica that Janet attended early in 2006 with the Breathing Project, a studio near her home. "From all this," Janet says, "I've learned to set limits with my mom—such as doing no more than one thing for her each day, and refusing to talk when I'm busy with my own work or social schedule. Like they say, you have to put the oxygen mask on yourself first."

What about intimacy in Janet's life? Given that her grandmother lived until Janet was well into her adult life and that the two were so close, an interrogator questions whether there was pressure for her to marry. "Yes," Janet says, "Grandma would say that it's not good to be alone. And when I reached the age where the child-bearing years were waning and I was feeling frustrated about probably never having children, she would say, very straightforward, 'You can always adopt.' And, who knows, maybe I will."

"Being single isn't a clear-cut issue," Janet states. "I don't say they set me on the road to being single, but witnessing the difficulty of my parents' marriage, I think I did absorb a lot of fear about intimate relationships that I continue to sit with and observe. I'm pretty sensitive to the power struggles and emotional strains that can come with romantic love. I don't trust easily, and when I do trust I have a habit of getting too focused on the person in question."

At forty-three, Janet believes that she is now in the place she needs to be in order to learn the lessons she is meant to learn. It is clear that, for her, yoga is a powerful and sustaining force. "Most of us are doing everything under the sun to squirm away from the truth of a given moment. When it comes to feelings of discomfort and pain, the more you try to avoid them, the more they push back and the harder it is to get the message they're sending. I need to hear—and heed—those messages.

"Even if society tends to pressure us into thinking so, I don't believe that people who are married have fuller lives. I don't think I'm necessarily more lonely because I'm single, or that I have to 'manage' being alone in any particular way.

"Maybe I will find a partner in this life with whom I'll share both love and marriage, though it still feels foreign to me. Whether there's a close relationship in my future or not, I would want to be able to accept the situation for what it is…and not wish it to be something else. I think my grandmother would appreciate my feeling strong enough to live my life this way."

◆   ◆   ◆

Recalling the time when Janet was a magazine's managing editor, Jinny St. Goar, one of her contributors, writes: "Almost single-handedly, Janet put out a magazine that swelled to one hundred twenty pages a month. She had a stable of writers but quite frequently during her years at the helm, she generated many of the story ideas, assigned them to writers, and edited the copy into publishable shape—all on her own. And somehow, through all the pressure, she maintained a sense of humor and a capacity to create and sustain friendships with her writers. She was encouraging and exacting, and a pleasure as a boss."

Becoming a Small Town Activist: Tom Wilkinson

Most large city dwellers rarely experience any sense of impact on the place where they live. That is not true for Tom Wilkinson. For him, life in the East Texas town of Mt. Vernon, population 2,300, means more than just avoiding big city traffic (though that is not an insignificant advantage). With his six-foot-two-inch lanky frame, moustache, scant hair, and Texas drawl, habitually turned out in cap and jeans and long-sleeved shirt, he can hardly go anywhere in Mt. Vernon without seeing someone he knows or, just as likely, who knows him. Simply by the identification between his recent forefathers and the place he calls home, Tom profits from an ongoing connection with the town, enjoying a certain status and perhaps even a key to escaping aloneness as a single man in his early seventies.

"The first moment of consciousness I had about the significance of the Wilkinson name in this community," Tom says, "came after my father's death in 1989 when his will was being probated in the Franklin County courtroom. Above the bench was a large photograph of my grandfather, the district judge. Both before and since that time, many people have shared their recollections of him with me. More and more I came to realize that he and his law practice, which lasted some seventy years, epitomized a time when lawyers ranked with ministers and doctors as the most highly respected men in their community—times when it really wasn't about money, when it was about public service. I think my grandfather stood for all the virtues of the old-time small town lawyer who tried to do the best for his community."

The elder generation of Wilkinsons passed on, though not before Tom's grandfather, the judge, reached 101, his father eighty-seven, his Aunt Agnes ninety-five, and his Aunt Gladys ninety-three. Being both an only son and grandson and without children of his own, there will be no one surviving Tom with his family name. He, therefore, has decided to make his own contributions to ensure that the Wilkinsons and the example his grandfather set aren't gone forever from their town. He has donated money for the Wilkinson Library at the Franklin County Historical Museum dedicated to the memory of his grandparents, a library that contains Texana and local history books and materials. He has also established the Wilkinson Gallery at the Old Jail Art Museum, dedicated to the memory of his Aunt Gladys, whose estate spawned artistic endeavors begun there in 1997. And thanks to Tom there will be an Agnes Wilkinson Burns Scholarship at the school where his aunt taught piano for over seventy-five years. "All of this," he says, "has become part and parcel of the legacy I want to leave to this area."

Having time now to spend as he wishes, Tom takes breakfast with other Mt. Vernonites at a local truck stop. But his mornings aren't spent just chatting over coffee on forays into town. He devotes hours as a volunteer in Mt. Vernon's downtown beautification, historic preservation, cultural enrichment, and library work, tasks that he claims to find extremely rewarding and that, by his own admission, make him a "big frog in a small pond." The two activities that have been most meaningful to him relate to his interest in art and decoration. "One is my involvement in the creation of the art museum in our historic old jail, the other the restoration of a house that belonged to a pioneer Confederate citizen, a project of the local historical association. I was able to pretty much charter the direction of the interior of the house, how it was furnished, and how it was arranged." The art arrangement aspects of projects, he claims, are the things he likes to do best and probably does best. "If I started over again," he says, "I would certainly go into interior design."

There's also the town square with the fountain and gazebo and landscaping put in years ago by The First National Bank. Mt. Vernon is lucky to have a park literally in the middle of the square, Tom explains, since in most East Texas communities that are county seats, it's the court house that gets situated there. "The beautification of the plaza downtown is the only project I actually originated," he says. "In 1982 the square was badly neglected and there was a feeling that the flower beds might just be best covered with gravel. I sort of spearheaded the movement to save the beds, and we started a volunteer project to keep them up. It has all improved, but with a sprinkler system that covers only part, other parts have to be watered by hand. We're limited as to the number of volunteers, and it's never really taken off as volunteer work. I go there myself but not as much as I should." According to Tom, it's general apathy or simply lack of vision that have held back the town projects that he supports.

Looking comfortable in a place he cares about and knows well, Tom adds, "I'm not sure Mt. Vernon is a typical small town anymore. Since the development of nearby Lake Cypress Springs over the last thirty years, it has changed a lot. There are people who have come here to get away from one thing or another, and those 'outsiders' have given the county a different sort of persona. I have friends from California, Iowa, Indiana, Florida, and Wisconsin in addition to the natives. There's a strong sense of community, and that includes more single people living happily here than you might expect. Most of those who grew up here don't perceive anything 'special' about Mt. Vernon or the county. It's the newcomers, like a fifty-three-year-old man who recently relocated from Hollywood, who arrive here and are absolutely charmed. 'It's like Mayberry,' says that newcomer, 'only better.'"

◆   ◆   ◆

Even with a family that is something of a brand name in Mt. Vernon, Tom is a unique presence, being a lifetime bachelor who describes his social life as "quite limited and very selective." He does not often go out in the evenings, times when many others like to mingle. It's by day that he generally connects with fellow Mt. Vernonites, and even those connections are limited. "My preferred socializing involves only one or two or three other persons in situations like tea or lunch or brunch," he says. "I don't seem to have a lengthy tolerance for most people."

Tom Wilkinson has had a lengthy tolerance for me, because (full disclosure) he and I have known each other since third grade, when we both entered Bradfield School in a Dallas suburb. Tom and his family had just moved from Mt. Vernon so that his father could practice law in the office of a major oil company in Dallas. My family and I had moved from South Dallas to a new part of town. Tom and I enrolled in Bradfield at the same time, and perhaps our friendship was struck from our mutual newness in the neighborhood and the school. In any case, it has survived six decades, during most of which we have lived hundreds of miles apart. For the time I lived in Dallas he was my only close non-Jewish friend. (For many years I called him Tommy, and it took some determination to let that be scaled back to a more grownup Tom.)

While I strayed north after high school, he remained south. In time his father retired from the oil company, allowing him and Tom's mother to return to their roots in Mt. Vernon. By then, Tom had acquired a bachelor's degree and three master's degrees and was working as a library consultant in a community college in Dallas. He counted on an inheritance that would come through at any moment, so at age fifty he quit his teaching post and, with it, life in Dallas. Packing up, he joined his parents as a returnee to Mt. Vernon. Now, when he revisits the big-city congestion in Dallas, one hundred miles to the west, he is pleased to have bucked today's trend of moving from small town to large.

Finished, he thought, with schools, he indulged an old fancy and opened a small, sophisticated antiques shop, a shop of the sort unfamiliar to Mt. Vernon. It was around that time that the bank mentioned above financed the building of a fountain and landscaping for the town's square. "I always associate Tom with the fountain and the square," says the current bank president, "since Tom's shop faced the fountain." Unfortunately, as Tom and the banker concur, a rural community like Mt. Vernon wasn't ready for a store filled with pricey fine pieces, void of junk. "It was ahead of its time," they say, and after three years, its uniqueness and a poor economy forced Tom to close it down. "Today it might survive," says Tom ruefully, "but not then."

Because of the Wilkinson family's trait of living into age late eighties and more, Tom's expected inheritance was not yet at hand, so without enough savings, he had to resume his teaching career, this time at Northeast Texas Community College, newly opened in 1985 in open land twenty miles from Mt. Vernon. It became the first community college in East Texas. "Northeast was exciting for me because I was there virtually at the beginning, and also because, for the first time in several years, I was not working in a library capacity," Tom says. "I was back into full time teaching and in three different disciplines: English, Art History, and Humanities. Humanities was particularly fun because I taught an interdisciplinary course that included music, art, and theater."

But, Tom says, starting a career again at age fifty-four wasn't easy, especially as he'd been living the ideal life for three or four years in what he says was really a play job as shop keeper. He stayed at Northeast for nine years teaching full time, and after one more year teaching part-time, he retired for good in 1995 at age sixty-four.

◆   ◆   ◆

Tom Wilkinson is really Richard Thomas Wilkinson III. The first, his district judge grandfather, lived in a splendid Colonial Revival house with a sweeping front porch on a corner of Mt. Vernon's Main Street. It was where Tom's father and his Aunt Agnes and Aunt Gladys were raised and where Tom also later lived until he realized that, though handsome and gracious, the house required upkeep out of proportion to the satisfactions it offered. He sold it a few years ago to a family just coming to town. In 2004, a hundred years after it was built, the house could have qualified for Texas landmark status, but its new owners wiped out that possibility by undertaking considerable renovations (not restoration, Tom carefully points out).

Now, in a newer section away from the center of town, Tom lives alone in a two-bedroom zero lot-line house with less character and less space but less upkeep than the old Wilkinson home, a relatively recent construction where rotting porches and foundations don't yet generate concern. On the outside of Tom's house are a covered porch and a thoughtfully-designed small garden with a narrow stone walkway and tiny fountain in the rear. Inside is a meticulously planned clutter of books, pictures, photos of family and friends, and carefully selected furnishings, some family possessions from a century or more ago, some new from today. Though it's a house suited for two, the interior seems arranged for the unshared lifestyle of one. What might serve as a guest bedroom has become an office. Through a rear window in Tom's back bedroom is a large pasture populated with a few cows living lazily under a huge, peaceful Texas blue sky.

A few years ago, the local newspaper ran an article on Tom, characterizing him as "a Renaissance man." Though he claims to be cleaning out possessions, he continues to add to his home library, already stocked with volumes ranging from architecture to history to art. An avid reader, he undertakes ambitious texts, including all volumes of Proust's *Remembrance of Things Past* and Dostoevsky's *The Brothers Karamazov*.

Considering his multiple degrees and refined taste, one might imagine that even sporting a distinguished family lineage, Tom would be out of place in a town of 2,300. That would be a mistake. Two decades after resuming life in Mt. Vernon, Tom acceded to a restless nature and began to consider returning to the Dallas area. As a trial, he bought a small house in a new development in McKinney, a far northern suburb of Dallas. "What I discovered after a couple of years of commuting between both towns was that for me, seventy was too old to start over in a strange place," he says. "So I sold that house and began to count my blessings here in Mt. Vernon." "Dallas," he tells me, "is no longer the city we grew up in, anyway."

Without seeking an active social life, Mt. Vernon provides Tom with as much privacy and anonymity as he wishes. "I'm an early morning person and don't like parties and seldom go to them, unless I have to," he says. "I do enjoy going to town in the morning and 'visiting' with the locals, but on my terms, that is, with limited intimacy." By early afternoon, Tom often retreats home, content to stay put for the rest of the day. In recent years, he owned three cocker spaniels, but they died one by one and have left him with no obligations to pets. Even so, he says that his visits to the local cemetery are to see the graves of Jacques, Peppe, and Brandon as much as those of his parents.

On trips to Mt. Vernon, I've accompanied Tom for his morning forays to the truck stop. There he puts away his cultured background along with his cap and merges with the local crowd. His clothes and pick-up truck are part of the merger, but so is the manner of speech, the Texas twang, slow and unhurried, a fact that jumped out at me some years ago when he and I took a long car trip together. We started from my territory in New York and made our way gradually to his (and, formerly, mine) in Texas. Did I notice a slight but unmistakable change in his speech pattern, becoming more southern, with more syllables per word ("yes" into "ye-e-es") as we went farther away from Yankee land? Yes. The sentences came out elongated, with a pronounced use of "ma'am" ("ma-a-m") and "sir," forms of address which cause someone to look skeptically if used in the North and which I didn't hear from him when we were North. Then there is southern lingo, phrases like, "I feel like I'm taking a cold," to which I have to resist the temptation to ask, "Where to?"

(That speech pattern isn't exclusive to Tom's generation. Not only did he refer to his father as "my daddy," I remember hearing his father, as an elderly, reserved man refer to *his* father as "my daddy.")

◆   ◆   ◆

Being the only person in line for an inheritance from older members of a family carries no few benefits, but responsibilities can also enter the mix. Tom had returned to living in Mt. Vernon just as the older generation of Wilkinsons reached a stage of limited mobility. To add to the problem, Tom's mother died unexpectedly of heart failure in 1976 at age seventy-four, leaving his father a widower and Tom in charge of his care. "Mother was gone and I had to take over my father's business affairs plus those of Aunt Gladys," he says. "Until then, I'd never really had to worry about anyone but me. Then, all of a sudden, I had to be concerned about these others. That required qualities for which I'd never been known, a sense of discipline and patience, especially since it wasn't long before I was back teaching again. In fact, I had a wonderful support system so that I really managed their care more than doing the caring myself."

With the long line of elder Wilkinsons gone and being now firmly settled in Mt. Vernon, Tom looks back over his lengthy work situations, residence in contrasting places, and close family involvements. His father's and grandfather's careers in the law failed to serve as a temptation for him. "I never really interacted with my father or his father, and in fact, when I was young, the dominant family influences in my life were female, not male. I was very strongly connected with my aunts, who cared for virtually nothing but music and art. That's when I formed my interest in the arts, which is the most important single thing in my life today. Ironically, if I'm trying to emulate anyone in my family, it's my grandfather, not because of the law but in the sense of community work, an interest that he passed on to me even though it skipped my father."

Despite their pursuit of music and art, Tom's aunts were small town women who were expected to marry, take a back seat to their husbands, and have no consuming career. "They were ahead of their time," Tom says, "because they flaunted those conventions, or at least didn't follow them, except to marry. In my opinion, the husbands of my aunts Agnes and Gladys were merely appendages to their lives."

◆   ◆   ◆

By his own admission, the person with whom Tom allowed himself the greatest intimacy, also female, was neither mother nor aunt, but Virginia Doss, a black woman who came to work for Tom's grandparents in 1943 and essentially stayed until she died half a century later. On visits to Mt. Vernon, Tom made sure that I had a chance to greet Virginia, a gracious elderly lady who then occupied the guest house built for her behind Tom's grandfather's house on Main Street. "In the beginning, Virginia assisted my grandmother in cooking and cleaning," Tom says. "But my family was classically Southern and matriarchal, and once my grandmother was gone, Virginia took her place, much as 'Mammy' did in *Gone With the Wind*." Remembering back to that time, Tom chuckles and adds, "After I returned to Mt. Vernon, my friends from Dallas came to visit and observed that my family did not seem to know that the Civil War had ended and slaves had been freed. Virginia had graduated into a role of domestic doyenne and did virtually everything for the helpless Wilkinsons except chew their food for them."

But Tom's relationship with Virginia started much earlier, when as a child he would go from Dallas to spend summer vacations at his grandparents' house. He avoided hearing grown-up talk of law and music by hanging out in the kitchen listening to Virginia. After picking up his residence in Mt. Vernon as an adult, he says, Virginia became an escape valve and the buffer between him and his family with their illnesses and high expectations. She was the person he could count on to make his life "work," especially within the context of a small town.

That ended in 1992 when Virginia was put in a hospital with an infected diabetic sore, never to come home again. "I visited her at Baylor in Dallas," Tom says, "then after several months of recovering from a stroke, she was moved to a nursing home in Mt. Pleasant, near Mt. Vernon." By that time, Buffy, Tom's female cocker spaniel, had replaced him with Virginia in her affections, so he would wrap Buffy in a blanket and sneak her in for a visit.

Virginia's death in 1993, Tom recalls, "spelled the end of my Mt. Vernon family life, because she was, in effect, the center of it, more than I realized during the time she was alive. She was irreplaceable. I had always brought her a piece of costume jewelry after my trips to thank her for taking care of the dogs. After she died, I took one of those rings and placed it on her white-gloved finger before the funeral."

Virginia is buried in the city cemetery with her own parents, but even now, Tom says, "it seems to me as if it would have been more appropriate if she were in the Wilkinson plot, beside Buffy and Jacques and Peppe who loved and missed her so much."

◆   ◆   ◆

Tom is old enough to reflect on what it is to be a senior citizen living alone in a small town. Aside from his volunteer work, he has adapted to his lifestyle a long-standing pattern of close relationships with couples. "I don't want to call it intimacy," he says, "but befriending married couples is a comfortable and secure way for me to be close to both male and female—physically even—without being deeply emotionally or sexually involved with either one."

Then there were the pets. "Until I had the dogs, and I didn't start having them until middle age, I didn't realize how much they could deflect the feeling of being alone. But dogs get extremely attached to their owners, and the smart ones I've had played on my needs to the point where I felt guilty about leaving them alone. The more I had to leave them, when I was still going to work, the less I could deal with it. So the companionship they offered was offset by my excessive anxiety and worry, and probably too much possessive love."

Now, Tom says, "I've made my particular peace with being alone. I think part of it is certainly situational, but another part has come with the realization that this is maybe the way I wanted it all along, and I allowed myself to be frustrated for years by thinking I had to be something else, I had to be intimate with people in a conventional way. My ability for that goes only so far."

If he shuns intimacy, Tom says it's at least partly because, as a child, he grew to view intimacy as something smothering, something to avoid. "That was primarily because my mother (in attempting to compensate for my father's distancing) offered too much intimacy, and I grew to find it, especially with a woman, as something that could 'swallow me up.' I've found it safer if the woman in question was romantically and/or sexually unavailable, at least in theory. If a husband was involved, I never had to worry about the relationship with the woman going too far, because if I liked the husband too (as I often did), I didn't want to be a home wrecker.

"With all that, there was a long time when I operated on the assumption that nothing would satisfy me short of an individual partner to live with. It has taken years, and a lot of those were unhappy years, but when I finally realized that I wasn't going to *let* it happen, for whatever reason or reasons, it stopped being such an issue and I started looking for things other than love interests. That didn't come from any 'how-to book,' just from years of looking outward and inward. If how I am today hasn't been a conscious choice, it's been a definite unconscious one."

Better than it might have worked in years past, Tom finds that his small town community-engaged but solitary lifestyle is fine for him today. "Maybe," he says, drawing a deep breath, "many of us don't want to live alone even when we know we should."

◆   ◆   ◆

I, this book's author, step in here as Tom's friend of many decades. He has surprised me by having no small mind but making a good life in a small town. He inherited an important name in Mt. Vernon but has more than given back to his town of his generosity and taste. Mt. Vernon has been lucky to have him, and I've been lucky to have had such an enduring friendship.

Managing as a Single Working Mother: Shelley Kern

There is little that's as hard as being a single working mother, believes fifty-seven-year-old Rochelle Kern (who everyone calls Shelley). Shelley and her second husband, Peter, lived together for seven years starting in 1977, but they separated in 1984 after less than three years of marriage. Their son Zach was eighteen months old. From then until recently, when Zach reached his early twenties, it was Shelley who, with occasional visits from Peter, raised their son alone. In those nearly two decades, she moved from New York to California and pursued different full- and part-time careers to support Zach and herself.

"Our son doesn't know anything other than having single parents; he has no memory of Peter and me being together," says Shelley. And in fact their marriage did not last long. "The baby's birth produced a new situation with my husband. Peter wanted to be first in my life while I was taking care of an infant—and he wasn't. He became increasingly possessive and I became increasingly unhappy. Our marriage had been brief, but I asked for a separation. Peter said that either we stay together or we divorce. That became the end of the marriage for me. I chose door number two."

Like any single parent, Shelley says that after leaving her husband, she shouldered the responsibilities that would otherwise be shared between two. "Zach was my priority and I was never ambivalent about that. I worked purposefully at part-time jobs so that I could be home every evening for supper with him." There were sacrifices, mostly giving up occasional job opportunities, but that was her choice.

In looking back, Shelley says that she found unexpected enjoyment in raising her son as a single mom. "There were drawbacks in being single, of course, but I found advantages also. I had no need to relate to a mate or a husband, in which I wasn't very successful or happy anyway, so I could focus on Zach through his childhood. Until he was eleven and we moved to California, he and I lived in Park Slope, a lovely neighborhood in Brooklyn. I had a wonderful group of friends who sort of adopted him and shared my job as parent. We would all meet and spend weekends at the Brooklyn Children's Museum or in Prospect Park. He got to appreciate the diversity of New York City."

Shelley admits to a tendency to overdo parenting and that only as she has gotten older has she managed to move away from it. That trait does not seem to have played negatively into her role as Zach's mother, however. "Zach reached the age of twenty-two in the year 2005," she says, "and for the first time he's functioning on his own as a young adult. I worried when he was younger about what would happen to him if I were to die. Now, no matter what happens to me, I know he'll be fine. He's a gifted musician, he's in a great music school here in Los Angeles and was one of two performers chosen to start in the school's year-end program in 2005. He's living with—and for the first time, really establishing a relationship with—his father. I'm altogether happy with that.

"I'm hoping that some of the hard work of raising a son is behind me, and now it'll be mostly fun. I'm still Zach's mother and happy to be, but no longer do I have to plan my life around caring for him. When he moved in with his father, I gave up a large space near Santa Monica. It was a relief not to need a big nest for the two of us."

Shelley's marriage to Peter ended in 1984, far enough in the past that she has had time to reconsider both that institution and the unpartnered life. "I've had several affairs since then," she says, "but today I share an apartment with Zelda, my cat, and that's enough. While I love being with Zach and others in the family, too, and I know how supportive family can be, when night comes I need my own time and my own space.

"I know it's not true for every mother, but even when Zach was a baby, I sought separate time to be by myself. It seems to be a constitutional requirement that no matter what I've been doing or whom I was with, at the end of the day I need to be alone for an hour or two—physically, quietly away from others.

"Being with a husband while keeping my own integrity was hard for me. I had time in two marriages to learn a lesson from my tendency to play the part of the parent. The lesson is that my happiness and even my good health come from living alone. When my own needs remain unfulfilled, I get unhappy and lose a lot of weight. It happened in my first marriage when I went down to about a hundred pounds. After my second marriage, after Peter and I split up, I knew I'd remain a single mother and never again live with a mate whether in love or lust.

"I never really missed Peter. Of course, whenever he and I go to something for Zach, we sit together. After all, we're his cheering section. We do agree on that."

◆   ◆   ◆

Shelley's wish to live by herself is at the end of process that started with a close-knit family in Southern California, perhaps too much so, according to her. Holding an unofficial doctorate in "Extended Family" earned from having two former husbands, a few ex-lovers, one sister, a natural son, five stepchildren plus many step-grandchildren, and a flock of twenty first-cousins plus their spouses, she is no stranger to close relationships. But it hasn't all been positive.

"My parents had a loving marriage for almost sixty years, but my mother suffered from clinical depression most of her life, and her needs were what ran the household," Shelley says. "Boundaries and roles that healthy families maintain weren't there with us. Mother might stay in bed all day with the curtains drawn, and my dad seemed always to be trying to nurture her. That threw me from an early time into the role of caretaker—of Mother, my dad, my sister, plus me. Since Mother was psychologically absent for my sister, who's two years younger than me, it was I who mothered her. Those were days when I should have been a child, not a mom.

"From the day I graduated high school in San Diego until I moved in with Morris, my first husband, five years later, I lived alone and enjoyed it immensely. I think it was our family situation at home that drove me out of the house so young. Oddly, that time of living by myself gave me a sample of the life I have now, years later."

But between those early days and today, relationships with two husbands or future husbands accounted for some thirteen years of Shelley's life. "Morris was more than twenty years my senior," says Shelley. "When we were first together, I was just twenty years old and he was forty or forty-one with four children by a previous marriage. He was wonderfully supportive while I was in graduate school, but I think the difference in our ages and my trying to play a mother's role and where we were in life all took a toll on the marriage. I wasn't able to articulate it to myself, but I was increasingly unhappy.

"One day I realized that I seemed to have outgrown him and I didn't have to stay. So I left him, though I was stuck carrying a lot of guilt. For a long time, Morris hung on to the idea of my coming back, and that pushed me to seek an official divorce. He has since passed away. Our relationship didn't end well, but there is one good thing, and it's that today his children and I are close."

"The odds were against both my marriages because I unconsciously carried over into them that mothering role I'd learned at home," says Shelley. That meant falling into the lives of her husbands, an arrangement that may have been nice for them but that left her with her needs and her happiness on hold. "It was easy for me to get overly involved in being the caretaker," she says. "I never managed to achieve a balance in caring for me while having a loving relationship with another person."

As a rebellious child, Shelley recalls, her role models were women of the old Wild West "I always loved and wanted to join the women of Rock n' Roll and the Blues before them. They were women who strived for equality and independence and political freedom." The star example in her own family was her grandmother's sister, Aunt Hinda, a Communist and midwife Russian immigrant. "Grandma was embarrassed by Hinda because she had pictures of Stalin and Lenin on the wall. Hinda was the black sheep of the family, but she was the one I really enjoyed. Growing up, people typed me as the hippy and said, 'Oh, you're like your Aunt Hinda.'"

Shelley also credits her father for instilling in her a strong belief in social justice. "My father was an incredibly decent man who was practicing civil rights issues as early as the 1940s because he believed that was just the right thing to do. He chose an African-American man as his tennis partner when partnering like that was segregated where they lived in Ohio. Maybe because of him—and Aunt Hinda too—I started doing civil rights organizing when I was fourteen and went to civil rights camps beginning a year later. I've always worked at jobs that were, themselves, political. The work I do has to be somehow meaningful to me. Today, I'm far to the left of most people and I'll probably die that way."

A spry five-foot-five inches tall, Shelley has a teenager's figure and seems right in an ankle-length skirt and loose blouse, a carryover look from her civil rights protest days. Age has given up any notion of curbing her energy. She seems strikingly untroubled, perhaps even thriving, by the continuing merry-go-round that has characterized her personal and professional life, which has caused her to move from California to New York City and back again. Even there, she has revolved between the western and eastern ends of Los Angeles.

"I was the first person in my family to go to and graduate from college," she says, "and I never dreamed of being more than a teacher or social worker. But friends encouraged me to continue in school, and I eventually received a Ph.D. in Sociology at the University of California at San Diego."

That was the beginning of transcontinental shuttling. "I was less interested in academic sociology than in the medical and psychiatric part, gender included," Shelley says. "In 1976, I received an offer to teach at New York University. My five years with Morris had ended and I was free to travel, so I grabbed the chance.

But when I started at N.Y.U., I discovered that I wasn't happy with straight sociology; I was more interested in the causes of illness than in theoretical discussions. That led me to a teaching fellowship at Columbia University and a Master's in Public Health."

Shelley says that, in time, she realized that she missed her family and the warm weather, and she really wanted to move back to the West Coast. By then she had married Peter and been divorced. "But I wasn't totally my own boss as Zach's mother. As part of the divorce from Peter, I had had to agree not to move my son out of New York State. Later, when Zach was about nine, Peter became involved with a woman in Los Angeles and wanted to move there himself. That made him more agreeable to my moving, too. He said that if I could find a job in Los Angeles, he would pay for our move. I grabbed at that offer."

In 1994 Shelley was hired as curriculum director in the Physician's Assistant program at the University of Southern California. After twenty years of New York life, she and Zach moved west, with Peter financing the move. "If we were going to move," Shelley says, "I wanted to do it before Zach was so old that it would be traumatic for him; he was already eleven, and the transition actually was tough for him. But my parents were in Los Angeles, I was able to spend their last years with them in a positive way and have Zach also gain some security from an older generation of our family."

Shelley learned that part of a mother's job is to understand a kid's changing mood. Peter's occasional return trips to New York didn't alleviate Zach's feeling of abandonment which persisted as long as they were there. Yet, once in California, where his father lived, Zach missed New York and was angry at his parents about why they had left the East. Shelley admits to occasional ambivalence herself about the change. "Much as I wanted to be back in California, a part of me missed and still misses New York City, which exerts such a strong pull on people. Mostly, it's my friends there whom I miss and the fact of public transportation that makes having a car unnecessary. There's so much the city can offer, a lot of it free or cheap."

Recently Zach went back by himself to live and work full time for several months in Manhattan. Shelley says that the experience made him realize that it was his childhood he had been missing rather than New York. "I was glad that he went and he had that realization." He returned to live in Los Angeles in 2004.

◆   ◆   ◆

Shelley's move back to California opened her to a troubled time profession-
ally. She ended up doing a job that previously had been done by three people,
and she was working under a department head at U.S.C. who was stealing tuition
dollars. When she eventually became a whistle-blower and went to the administration to complain about the thefts, she and two other senior faculty members
were fired. "When you work in a medical school, you work at the whim of the
administration," she explains. "We were not on a tenure track."

Shelley says that she was exhausted and unhealthy by the time she left U.S.C.
in 2002. For the next three years, she had to support herself and her son with
part-time work. "That certainly had its effect on Zach; it didn't make my role as
single mother any easier either. He saw, and I experienced, how hard it is to be
hired in a new job at age fifty-seven, even if you're a person with great qualifica-
tions." In spring 2005 luck came her way. She connected with the Emperor's
College of Traditional Oriental Medicine in Santa Monica, where she began to
teach research methods part time in their graduate programs. Soon she was hired
as their full-time academic dean.

Shelley smiles as she says, "That college provides a kind of social good that I
believe in. They have trained and licensed acupuncturists for twenty years in a
master's clinical training program. Now they're establishing a new doctoral program." There are four hundred students in the master's program, and Shelley is
in charge of all the classroom education they receive. "There are administrative
responsibilities, but I have some help on those. Best of all is that I teach research
methods in the efficacy of oriental medicine in the new doctoral program. It's in
teaching that I feel the most fulfilled. If someone asks what work I do, I always
say that I am a teacher."

Shelley finds her new connection a great match for her and her for it. "I've
always been somewhat outside of the medical model, critical of bio-medicine,
especially as it's practiced here in the West. Oriental medicine is different; it
looks at individuals in the context of their entire lives, tries to understand a whole
person and then makes a diagnosis and a plan for treatment. Increasingly, Western medicine and bio-medicine are reaching toward oriental medicine, especially
acupuncture. It doesn't hurt you, and it works!"

Geography takes a role in the story. In 2004 Shelley left her home in Santa
Monica and moved to Los Feliz, an area of East Hollywood with less traffic than
the "heartland" of Hollywood and what she calls "a wonderfully, ethnically

mixed population." Shelley's abode was a second floor studio apartment big enough for her and Zelda and an accumulation of books and papers to do with work and family. It was in a small building that benefits from cheery sunlight with decent parking on the street and proximity to a busy shopping area.

But to commute from Los Feliz to her new work in the college in Santa Monica is "unbearably long," says Shelley—three hours round trip. So in true Southern California style, she has moved again to accommodate a job—her fourth change since returning to Los Angeles. Seeming unfazed by one more need to pack and reverse direction, she doubled back to Culver City in her old neighborhood to a two-bedroom rental apartment. Zelda of course was part of the convoy.

Shelley doesn't expect to call it quits to her own education. "I hope to return to school to obtain a license in Marriage and Family Therapy, partly because I really believe in its value and also to allow me to work for myself as much as I might want or need to in the future."

◆   ◆   ◆

"My life is changing," says Shelley, "and is not yet what I want it to be. Single people meet and bond in different ways in Los Angeles than in New York. I didn't have that trouble in the East, but I've found it hard to make new friends of my generation here. That's partly because, until recently, I was a full-time mom, which limits your free time. Also, at U.S.C., I was the boss, and as the boss you don't make friends. Plus I was working eighty to ninety hours a week."

Says the single mother, "I had mixed feelings about Peter's limited involvement with Zach, coming every so often back to New York from California to see him. But I was blessed that Peter was an occasional presence in my son's life and that he paid child support and school and medical expenses and summer activities. Peter is good with little kids but has difficulty with children once they're older, so it may be as much to his benefit as to Zach's that they're now living together. Ironically, having moved to California for a relationship, Peter's failed. He and I are both single today, though he is not happy with that situation.

"Without having to care for Zach on a daily basis, and with a new job that I hope will be more balanced, I'd like to have more time and a better social life."

That does not mean remarrying or even settling in with a lover, a plan that sets her apart from many other women. "I find few people who feel as I do about relationships, women especially, who always seem eager for the next husband or boyfriend or girlfriend. That's true for most of the women I know, straight or gay. I couldn't have that kind of life. I've had a lot of lovers and if I have another or don't have another, it's just not important. I think that what I miss most today is the company of women friends. I'd rather expand my network that way than to find another male friend.

"I have a son whom I've helped to raise and who's getting by on his own, a decent person I love and am proud of. A husband isn't necessary for me to feel fulfillment."

Shelley reverts to the subject of loneliness, so central an issue for many people who live alone. "Loneliness is something I rarely experience," she says. "I think one reason is that I've lived a lot internally and have always been comfortable in my own company. But there's even more to it. If I don't have time alone, I feel as if I'm coming unglued and, literally, can't fall asleep at night. It's a purely physical need.

"I recognize that people who enjoy the kind of life I seek are unusual. Others assume that I'm lonely and they worry that I'll be an old lady, alone. They don't get it. I say, 'If I'm an old lady alone, then that's what I'll be. I'm OK with that.' My anxiety turns out to be the opposite of many people who fear being alone or lonely. I have anxiety from not having that time by myself. I enjoy being with men but not for living with one again. That is a situation that leaves me feeling as if I'm suffocating. I'm not a person who's particularly pleasant when I'm intimately sharing a life.

"I know I'm different, and it becomes difficult to convince people who are sure that I must be miserable in my life. With a great job that's right for me, and a young-adult son—both of which make me very grateful—the news is that miserable I'm not!"

◆   ◆   ◆

Zachary Kern-Schnall, Shelley's son, writes: "My mom is very young at heart, very independent, brilliant, and somewhat stubborn. She allowed me to have the type of lifestyle I wanted, fun with friends and girlfriend without any real consequences. She's always been very loving, never have I doubted that, but sometimes I have doubted whether or not she was afraid to discipline me out of fear of rejection."

Finding Sanctuary in Music and Books: Glenn Raucher

Glenn Raucher, who is now the head of a four-person award-winning band, could rightly claim that his musical future got seriously derailed even before high school. Here's what happened.

At about age ten he was awarded use of the attic room in his family's house on Long Island. "I climbed the stairs up to the attic, closed the door, and was in my own world. It was pure joy," he says. "I already was spending time on my own because my younger sisters, twins, had each other, and I had…me. Upstairs I invented dice baseball games and began to write. Papers came flying out if you opened a drawer of my little kid's desk. People who knew me then have remarked to the adult me that I was 'such a serious child.'"

The attic room was where Glenn started to listen to music and to write lyrics, without a band to bring them to life. At thirteen, he happened to be given a record of a Canadian band called Rush. "Until that time, the music I listened to was whatever my parents listened to. But Rush was not like that…not like anything I'd heard…technical hard rock without being heavy metal. Their lyrics had meaning. They spurred me on to more writing, and when I was fourteen I found Clint Gascoyne, a friend with whom I could express the parts of me that meant something…the artistic part, the writing, the music."

So far, so nice. Here comes the bad part.

Glenn's parents bought him an inexpensive electric bass, and he joined two other boys to form a band in junior-high school. "I didn't have any lessons and they were older kids who, unfortunately, weren't going to teach me or allow me time to learn. They were playing other people's music, music that was hard to play. I wanted to write my own songs and sing them, and I tried to convince them that it was OK to do that."

But it didn't work. Glenn says his tenure with those two boys ended when they met a "junior delinquent" who claimed to sing and play bass, neither of which could he do. "But they thought he was cooler than I, so to make it impossible for me to stay around and even try to play, they took a screwdriver to my bass and destroyed it."

"Well," says Glenn today, "what do you think? I felt like shit, no surprise. But I'm glad it happened because it helped break the spell I was under. After all, those were people I thought were my friends!"

If Glenn became philosophical about that moment, as he says he did, he faced one more teenage setback. "Though I spent a lot of hours in the attic at home, I played sports with other kids, too. I *loved* playing them and I was good at all of them. Unfortunately, it didn't matter because I never managed to be accepted at part of the team. The guys in my neighborhood who I hung out with, again, were older, and if you were creative and at all comfortable with how you were and not pretending to be something else, it wasn't looked upon highly.

"I was part of a street hockey team, but some of the other boys formed a clique and left me out. I was just different from them, and my sensitivity made me an easy target. There came a day when we had a game, and I was expecting a car to come and pick me up. I was waiting outside all dressed for the game when the car drove by with the other boys inside, laughing as they left me there. Maybe it was just the cruelty of kids, but it was awful."

Both experiences, Glenn believes, forced him to find new friends and new ways to express himself. "I especially needed to lose the guys in that band. They would have been happy playing other people's songs for the rest of their lives. I wouldn't be."

The story gets better.

Glenn's breakup with the old band caused him to seek out people like his friend Clint. In fact, he says, if that early group had strung him along, maybe the depth of his relationship with Clint would have been missed. In high school the two formed their own band. "We called it Equilibrium. Clint wrote lyrics, I wrote lyrics, and we found someone who would write music. Yes, what I wrote were bad lyrics about things that were important to an eighteen-year-old, but they became the first true expression that I had artistically." (Today, Glenn reports, Clint Gascoyne is still his best friend and "the best drummer I've ever heard.")

Fast forward to 2006, where Glenn and Jason Staal are what Glenn calls "joint CEOs" of a four-member band called Home to Henry, created when the two met in July 2002. "Jason and I have been writing songs together since then," says Glenn, "and Home to Henry is now the three-time recipient of honorable mention in *Billboard* magazine's Song of the Year contest. We won once in 2003 for the song 'Feels Like Winter' and twice in 2004 for 'I Could Just Kiss You' and

'Tina.' We've recently recorded a CD called *Another Life*, which includes those songs in full-band versions."

Letting out a wry smile, Glenn confesses that in all these years he never learned to read music. "I was always 'just' the singer and lyricist, and it never became necessary to learn to read music, especially as we were playing rock, which rarely requires much reading."

Aside from Glenn and Jason, Home to Henry has Rob Holt and Jim Stellato. For two hours a week on Tuesdays they meet to play together as a band, but that doesn't account for the time Glenn spends thinking about it…which, he says simply, is "all the time." Besides playing, he sketches ideas for lyrics and deals with the business aspects of where to go after making the CD. "On that I collaborate with Jason because he and I are the bosses."

Teenage crises seem to have been the catalyst for coming back strong in Glenn's life. With a look that says he's glad to be past rejection by other boys on a street hockey team or in a junior-high band, but grateful for the moment he hit on the album of Rush, Glenn, at age thirty-eight, states, "I've found music to be the great healer. It became the sanctuary—it never judged me."

◆   ◆   ◆

Forty-five pounds lighter than he was three years earlier, Glenn resembles an engaging, bright-smiling graduate student, standing six-feet-two-inches tall and reed-slender in a black T-shirt, skinny black jeans, and close-cropped dark hair. But his responsibilities are the grown-up kind. Veering far away from music, a large part of Glenn's life unfolds at the West Side YMCA in Manhattan where he heads the Writer's Voice, a long-established New York City writing program.

Glenn followed a circuitous route to that job. Living alone since his divorce in summer 2004, he tells of having left New York to accompany his wife, Laura, a dancer, while she pursued a degree in Oregon. In 2000 they returned to New York after being gone for a decade. "We had no contacts here, no easy job to find. One of my mom's friends was the executive director of the East Side Vanderbilt YMCA, and she took me in as someone just to deal with organizing e-mails for reserving guest rooms.

"I was already thirty-four-years old and going to be an e-mail clerk! But I needed something to get my wife and me and our two cats out of my parents' house. It only took a week to get the e-mails straightened out, and then I moved to the front desk and became the de facto assistant manager and took over all the reservations."

When the West Side Y created the position of Guest Room Supervisor in January 2003, Glenn transferred across town to the neighborhood of Lincoln Center. It was, he says, with high hopes and a lot of ambition that he came, "but there weren't enough resources, not enough manpower, and the frustration of trying to do a job at one level having only the tools to do it at another level ate at me. Also, in February, I'd hurt my back following years of playing goalie in hockey and catcher in baseball or softball. I'd gotten to the point where I was bent over in half for most of the year. Plus, my marriage was ending."

Within a few months, Glenn was seeking employment elsewhere. At that moment, the position of Literary Arts Coordinator at the Y opened up. "I'd been wanting to get back into the arts, and here was a job in a building where I was already working. Because room rentals account for millions of dollars in revenue at the Y, the salary was going to be several thousand dollars less than that of the Guest Room Supervisor. But I didn't care. I love the arts…and it would be a decrease in stress."

Glenn took the job and has remained at the West Side Y. Since October 2003 he has been responsible for running the Writer's Voice, the Y's long-established writing program. He calls it a job that pays more than that of Guest Room Supervisor, but not with money. "My back feels better and I've never been happier at work. It took twenty years to find the thing that's meant for me."

The Writer's Voice offers year-around writing workshops in fiction, poetry, screenwriting, playwriting, memoir, journalism, and some multi-genre classes in fiction and non-fiction. "When I started in the job," says Glenn, "there was a defection of students and teachers and a tremendous suspicion here. The teachers had been through a difficult time, with promises made and, for whatever reason, not kept. Aside from recruiting students, I had to win over the faculty, gain their trust, and make them see that the program was going in a positive direction. Recently, one teacher who both left and returned told a number of students that she thought the program was back where it had been at its height."

Glenn reports that the sixteen Writer's Voice classes offered at the beginning of 2006 all had enrollments with a higher percentage of students than ever before. "We've never had such great enrollments in a non-summer session," he says.

There's still plenty to do. "I want the Writer's Voice to be part of the West Side community rather than just an aspect of the Y. And I'm advocating for proper salaries and budgets for the school's instructors." But the occasional great moment makes the effort worthwhile. "We had a student who took a memoir workshop and wrote a wrenching tale of an abused childhood and drug involvement. She asked an actress to come and read it to the class so that she could hear what it sounded like. At the end of this difficult and astounding evening, the student said, 'I didn't really believe it before…but I am a writer.' That made it worth every little headache."

The Writer's Voice sponsors a full calendar of authors' prose and poetry readings, and organizing that series is a job Glenn takes seriously, as I can testify from the opportunity I had to read there from a new novel in the fall of 2004. Unlike other hosts at similar events, Glenn had done a careful study of my book and led off a lively discussion afterward that engaged both the audience and me. Does he do that with all authors who come to read at the Y? "Yes," he says. "Writers value the fact that you've taken the time to read their book. I've been lucky and not picked up a book from any of our authors that has been a chore to get through."

While still working to build a large crowd, Glenn says that his objective with the readings is to make sure that the authors' books have been understood and that they have a good time when they come. "I want to make it more like, 'Oh, a writer happened to walk into our living room, so let's talk about his or her book.'"

"I begin to see other departments at the Y employing some methods that I've brought in," Glenn adds with a smile. "For the first time that it's really mattered, I feel appreciated in my job."

Different as it is from the world of music, Glenn is not a stranger to the world of books. "My family had great book collections, and my grandfather, especially, encouraged me to read what he had on the Civil War. I never got into the subject until years later, when I watched the Ken Burns's documentary, and then I went whole-hog into it. I've probably read three hundred books on the topic by now. But just having those books around made me curious and want to read, and I believe that led into my own writing. It's also made me appreciate what writers whom I meet at the Y go through."

◆   ◆   ◆

Camping out for a week in a barren western desert isn't likely to be everyone's ideal vacation, especially if it's their first one in nearly two years. But at the urging of a close friend, Glenn put the idea on his screen, then traveled across the country and made good on it for eight oven-like days in late August 2004.

The place was Black Rock, an immense stretch of northern Nevada desert, and the occasion was Burning Man, which calls itself "an annual experiment in temporary community dedicated to radical self-expression and radical self-reliance." Ready to practice community and self-reliance were some 35,000 adults and children from many states and several foreign countries who had come supplied with food, tents, water, and portable showers.

Challenges descended from day one, especially for big-city guys not experienced at survival in the outdoors, Glenn reports. "That first day for me was really difficult. Everyone was part of a small camp—ours had thirteen people—and while we were setting up tents and getting settled, I started feeling light-headed and had to stop for a couple of hours. It was very disheartening because when that happens, I'm the kind who feels he's let the others down, though they told me just to chill and look forward to the week ahead. The second day our camp was assigned to set up lights in a huge circle around the field. I still felt the effects of the hundred-degree afternoon, but I worked harder to make up for what I hadn't done the first day."

With challenges came compensations. "During that week I simply learned to do life differently, something I really needed to do," says Glenn. "That meant allowing myself to be spontaneous and unrehearsed and open to whatever happened. Nothing was scripted and nearly everything occurred at random. I spent most of my days walking around to meet others in camps set up in the circle." Unlike New York, where people strain to avoid eye contact, Glenn found that there was almost no one who wouldn't at least say hello and comment on the recent dust storm. Meetings often developed into real conversations.

Every kind of reason had brought people to Burning Man. Many were nearing a divorce or a significant breakup, and they went to seek clarity or peace. Some came to have a week's drug experience, some went for sex. Glenn says, "I did not rule out sex before I got there, but as soon as I arrived, I realized if that was what I was chasing, it would devalue my overall experience significantly."

As for why he did go, Glenn says, "I was having hell with my job, my marriage had fallen apart, and I'd exacerbated my back injury—debilitating emotional *and* physical stuff. I went with the hope that I could leave behind a lot of things in the desert—a mythical sort of idea.

"Something remarkable happened the first night there. Sitting outside our tent, I looked up and watched someone's rainbow kite floating amidst the panoply of stars that are so beautiful in the desert. I really felt as if there were parts of my brain that were being manually stimulated; it was a physical and mental sensation. There's no way to explain it, and I don't think I even need to, but a sense of the sorrow left and a weight came off me. For the first time in years I felt what I called 'unclenched.'"

Glenn says that when he finds himself retreating into the nervous, vibrating New York life, he reminds himself of how he was at Burning Man. "It doesn't always work," he says, "but I have the experience and know that it's possible to return to that feeling. I come back to it often during the day. My growing up was not wildly joyful, and sometimes I get the same feeling these days. That's why I'm so relieved when I just get a pure blast of inexplicable joy, as I did at Burning Man."

Today Glenn looks like the world's most unclenched man.

◆   ◆   ◆

Glenn characterizes himself as a person who thought that his role was to make things work for others, to do everything perfectly, and to feel inadequate when that didn't happen, as on the first day at Burning Man or at his first job at the West Side Y, or, indeed, in his marriage.

"I was married in June 1997, and the marriage lasted a little over six years. It ended with the most amicable divorce in history, with no children, no financial complications, and no recriminations. It ended despite both of us trying to keep the thing together, seeing a succession of counselors, even communicating well with each other. Laura, who is eight years younger than I, had always lived under the protection of her parents or roommates until we got married, and since I was already independent, all she had to do was step aboard. As the marriage went on, I was the initiator and she the receptor, which reinforced the imbalance in our relationship. We both recognized resentments rising up, and felt that we wouldn't be able to maintain the good between us. It was then we realized that going forward with a divorce was the only right thing to do. At that point, September 2003, my wife moved out.

"Laura and I are best friends—she will always be a part of my life—but it's not enough for a marriage. She doesn't have a bigger fan than I am, and I know that I was the first man in her life who really treated her well. She has another one now, and I can feel comfortable saying that I paved the way for that."

When his wife left, Glenn missed and does still miss coming home and being greeted with a hug. At the same time, he felt the relief that comes from an end to growing tension at home, a relief that he believes his wife must have shared. To help with the rent and fill both physical and psychic space, Glenn advertised and found a roommate. "The man moved into the spare room in November 2003," he says, "and it didn't take long to see that it wouldn't work for me. I wanted to share a little with another person, but I couldn't ask that of a stranger who was determined to stay a stranger. It was like having an alien presence, almost lonelier than being alone, because he was in the apartment but not part of it. I avoided the living room to watch the news if I knew he was there but didn't want to see it."

There was another separation when the roommate moved out, one Glenn says was in some ways more stressful than the separation from his wife. In fall 2004, bearing his two cats in hand, Glenn moved to a smaller apartment in the same building, singling him out as one of the extreme minority of New Yorkers who set out to gain less space.

◆   ◆   ◆

Besides the early years in his attic room, there was time between about ages twenty-five and twenty-nine, before his marriage, when Glenn lived alone. "And," he says, "I liked it." He's there again since his divorce but with knowledge gained about himself that makes his renewed single life different. Recognizing and attending to his own needs, something easy or natural for others but mostly foreign to him, has been a huge part of his growing. "Much as I was the initiator in our marriage, I was also the guy who would soothe my wife, never come out and say to her, 'I have a problem with X, because I'm not getting Y.' And I don't mean to imply that she was placing any limitation on what I did or when or where I did it. It was me doing that to myself out of some idea that I had to be the anchor of our relationship. I always thought that everyone else's needs were more important than mine and if everyone else was happy, then I'd be happy.

"I was wrong, and did a pretty good job of not showing the resentment I felt building up. That only meant I was poisoning myself more, and if the resentment ever did emerge, it was going to be ugly. My wife and I finally faced that, before it reached that point."

How does Glenn manage his single status today? He says that he tries to remain conscious of when he's beginning to feel isolated and takes steps from letting it become too much. "But," he adds, "I can be perfectly happy, very well satisfied, with a good book and a good restaurant. And I do like my smaller apartment, where every part of it is mine and where I can come and go as I desire."

He underscores the fact that he now knows the importance of caring for his needs. "This has come mostly from reflecting on my divorce, seeing that I had to, absolutely had to, make changes in how I perceived and did things. It's meant facing up to many things that I didn't like to face, doing a lot of 'onion-peeling.' Burning Man served in many ways as the culmination of that process, coming as it did nearly one year after my wife left."

Being in a good physical and emotional state is essential for leading a schedule as crammed as Glenn's. The band sometimes has to play backup to the Writer's Voice, work that he says he really loves. "If I throw myself into it and say that it's the job that saved my life, that's only a small exaggeration, considering what else was going on in my life. I feel so lucky to be back in something connected with the arts. This thing that just landed in my lap throws me challenges but also gives me affirmation eight hours a day, and I know how rare that is because I've been in jobs that made me feel terrible."

The authors' readings that Glenn organizes at the Y not only furnish him with good books to read and a connection to contemporary publishing but, as he jokes, provide him dates with anywhere from a dozen to fifty people a couple of nights a week year around. He also stays in frequent touch with his parents on Long Island and, by phone, with a host of friends all over the country.

While he puts himself out as a single man looking for a single woman, Glenn says that from his marriage he learned that simply having a relationship isn't the answer. "If there are holes to be filled, they have to be filled by me, without waiting for someone else to do it. Should there be a relationship along the way, great, but I won't wait for that to develop a full life day by day. I do set a high, high bar for myself."

There was a Sunday morning in summer 2004 when Glenn was scheduled to play in a softball game with some male friends. It was to follow a date the night before. "In my mind I went into the date saying, 'this is all well and good, but I'm playing ball tomorrow morning, and I'm gonna be there at 8:30 no matter how this evening goes. If it goes well, the person will understand that I'll be there for them when I'm with them.'

"I'm going to do the things that make me happy, because I have to believe that if I'm happy, someone else will recognize that."

◆   ◆   ◆

Glenn Raucher has permitted the reprinting here of the year 2004 lyrics he wrote for "I Could Just Kiss You," one of the songs recognized in *Billboard* magazine:

> I left the dust to settle
> after I cleared out the room

and the paint is still peeling
and the place is filled with you.

Chorus:

Gone are the days
When I would think
When I didn't know what to do:
I could just kiss you.
I could just kiss you.

Things drain into silence
and cold fills the room
and the cats are still crying
and the place is filled with you.
Your plants still on the window
a white dress hangs in the hall
and I wish that you would tell me
"it's just a ghost, that's all."

Chorus

Bridge:

I look to my left and you're not there
My hand doesn't rest on your shoulders
Fingers don't stroke your hair.

I look to my right and everything's wrong
No one to laugh at the just the right moment
No one to sing along.

Chorus

Back and forth like a timepiece
suspended on a chain

there's no clock to count the moments
'till I can have you again.

So when the dust is settled
And I've cleared out the room
The paint will still be peeling
And the place still filled with you.

Chorus

◆   ◆   ◆

Marcia Golub, an instructor at the Writer's Voice, says: "Glenn, you really are the reason this writing program is doing well. They tried to kill it before, but you have brought it back to life. You are full of great ideas and energy."

Combining Faith, Prayer, and Community: Nancy Kehoe

By the time the Christmas season arrives, nun and psychologist Dr. Nancy Kehoe has draped the living room of the community house where she lives in Cambridge, Massachusetts, with holly, bouquets of pine, and a splendidly decorated tree. Nancy shares the house with five other nuns, four in her religious order and one from a different congregation. The departure of the other sisters for their year-end family visits signals Nancy to set to work preparing a holiday evening for nine or ten of her friends not always associated with the church (in fact, mostly Jewish). On the night of the party, she welcomes them wearing a festive Christmas outfit, and she proffers appetizers and wine followed by an ambitious dinner menu at a long dining table embellished with candles and flowers. It has become an annual tradition that Nancy says she loves. "It's better to do the dinner when the others in the community are away," Nancy says, graciously. "They're all introverts."

That's something Nancy Kehoe isn't. (With her approval, she will be referred to here as Nancy.) A vivacious and attractive woman in her late sixties, Nancy's life in a religious order—it's called Religious of the Sacred Heart—began unplanned, even unwanted, when she was an eighteen-year-old freshman at a Catholic college in Nebraska. One evening, during a chapel service, she heard a sudden voice, presumably the voice of God, who said to her, "I want you to go to Kenwood." Kenwood, she knew, was in Albany, New York, the place where young women went to be formed as nuns.

Though she was from a devout Catholic family and her mother and grandmother were both educated by nuns, Nancy remembers that entering religious life was the last thing she expected or even wished for. "I hated the idea," she says, "and I burst out crying. But the voice was so explicit that I believed I should do it. 'Not my will, but thine be done,' I said, because doing God's will was all important in my family. I spoke to my aunt, who was then the president of the college, and she suggested that I stay in college one more year. But I told her that if I didn't enter then, I knew I wouldn't."

On a visit back with her family in Chicago, Nancy told her plans for entering religious life, and, she recalls, "my mother almost died. I was the only daughter. My aunt, Mother's sister, had already taken vows, and back then, in 1956, nuns in the order I was going to were cloistered. That meant that once they entered, they didn't go home again for any reason. Still, I believed I'd gotten a sign that this was what I should do."

She proceeded, but cautiously. "I was so doubtful about what lay ahead that I tried to squeeze every pleasure out of life between March and the time to go East," she says. That meant postponing telling anyone outside her family, including her boyfriend, whom she continued to date for several months. "I didn't really treat him very nicely by keeping from him what I was planning," she recalls with embarrassment. On the way to Albany in September, she even delayed her trip with a few days' stopover in Manhattan where she asked a friend to arrange a couple of blind dates for her. Her eventual arrival at the convent was unorthodox: in a slightly tipsy state following some rounds of big city partying.

After a couple of months at the convent, Nancy says she turned herself inside out and became utterly scrupulous about doing everything she was asked to do. That, however, followed her first days and weeks that she remembers as awful. "I hated it," she says. "I walked around wondering what I was doing there. There was a beautiful fall day when I wished I'd been in New York going to a West Point game." Young women entering the convent were given rules for everything they were to do or not do all day long. "The hardest by far," Nancy says, "was the rule of silence, which was imposed almost immediately after we arrived. We were allowed to speak only of things necessary, in the right place, at the appointed time, and in as few words as possible. If we wanted to have a conversation with a friend in the convent, we had to ask permission, and we were not allowed to talk about feelings or family or anything going on in the world, which we were kept from anyway. That left only pious things to discuss. Then 'grand silence' was enforced from nine o'clock at night until after breakfast the next morning.

"Besides the external regulations, there were internal admonitions, things we were not supposed to think about and things we could think about. Every single minute of our day was organized, even our free time. If we wanted to read a book, we had to ask permission of a superior. I worked so hard not to break the rules—more than a lot of other novices, I later found out. But being so conscientious also made me very anxious and troubled."

Even so, Nancy took her vows in time and then set out for the rest of her life as a nun in the order called Religious of the Sacred Heart.

Unlike others in this book who have come to an unpartnered life in a variety of ways, it was the very path on which Nancy set forth that required a life of remaining unpartnered, at least in the traditional sense. Meeting her today, one comes upon a woman busily committed to her own business, teaching, working in her community and her religious order, and keeping in close touch with family and friends, in all, a woman who emanates energy and fulfillment. One isn't likely to wonder if she questions the decision made following that moment in a chapel decades earlier.

But Nancy says that it has been a struggle. "The life I chose, with not being partnered, is a continuing sacrifice for me. I've done what I think God has asked me to do. If I hadn't heard that voice that was so emphatic, if I hadn't entered religious life, I'm sure I would have married and had children and by now probably grandchildren, as my two brothers have done. But that voice that said I was being called at eighteen was so strong—I hear it still.

"I think that probably what I most miss is the intimacy that can come from a marriage and the learning that derives from dealing with another person day in and day out—how someone maintains his or her own self while also being there for someone else. I look at my brothers and see the way they interact with their wives and what it has done for them as people. That kind of thing I envy."

◆   ◆   ◆

Nancy's challenge has been to bring devotion to a life not chosen without losing all her own identity. She's followed an intricate course, occasionally accidental, and today she views herself as more of a paradox than many nuns she knows. She recalls arriving at one of her jobs in a rented pick-up truck. "Also," she says, "I threw big parties for my fiftieth, my sixtieth, and my sixty-fifth birthdays! The sisters with whom I share the house came to the parties…but they would never have initiated them nor wanted anything similar for themselves."

The course she has followed started years ago, shortly after taking her vows. As an unsteady twenty-four-year-old, Nancy was sent to teach young girls at the order's school in Lake Forest, Illinois (where the rules of silence largely also held forth). "It was a really painful time," she says. "The youngsters picked up on how tense I was and really rode rough shod over me. Some time afterward, I learned that a lot of those girls were, themselves, disturbed. A disturbed teacher with disturbed kids wasn't a great combination. Years later, I bumped into one of my former students who told me, 'We really gave you a hard time!'" A convent school in Cincinnati was Nancy's next assignment, and there she enjoyed more success. In fact, she has remained friends with one of those girls whose wedding she later attended.

The year 1967 was pivotal for Nancy as for hundreds of nuns and priests. In amending the requirement that nuns be cloistered, the Catholic Church decreed that religious men and women working in active ministry—teaching or hospitals or orphanages—need no longer maintain a monastic life. That meant that nuns like Nancy were allowed to work in non-traditional settings, as she and her housemates now do. Neither were they henceforth required to wear religious habits. Nancy delayed changing to civilian clothes until three years later out of respect for the conservative atmosphere of Cincinnati. As important as were those changes, none surpassed her first joyous trip home to spend a snowy Illinois Christmas with her family. It was 1967, ten years after her entry into the religious order.

In 1970 Nancy moved to Boston to pursue a doctorate in psychology at Boston College. With the degree and after a year teaching at a Jesuit seminary, she started working at Cambridge Hospital. A psychiatrist whom she befriended there remembers that Nancy was thrown in with deeply disturbed patients. But the job became significant in ways she couldn't have expected. "I was amazed," says Nancy, "after my own years of religious life, to learn that no one in the hospital—or anywhere in the mental health field—mentioned anything about religion and spirituality when they talked to patients or about patients. It was as if the subject of religion had been considered by the medical community as more a symptom of the disease than a possible source of insight."

Nancy got labeled as something of a radical, but she began to raise the question of what it meant that this subject was so excluded. She started helping doctors to think of language to make it more comfortable for them to ask patients about God, or prayer, or anything in their religious past.

After awhile, Nancy says, she was asked to do a consultation at a day treatment program connected to Cambridge Hospital. At the end of the consultation, people on the staff who knew of her religious affiliation said that many of their clients talk about religion and that "we don't know what to do with it—so we ignore it." Nancy suggested that they form a group and that the group focus on religious issues. She says, "I think they were skeptical at first because they thought that religion was part of their clients' symptoms and their whole illness. But it became a start on exploring larger possibilities."

"I also joined a group called Psychologists Interested in Religion," Nancy goes on, "and because of that connection, I started to give presentations in different places. A Wisconsin mental health organization hired me to do training with their staff. That at first was to be a year's commitment, but I've been going there five years now and have trained about fifty staff persons in hospitals and day treatment centers."

And that is how she came to develop a consulting business called Expanding Connections. Frequent travel, which she loves, brings Nancy to different cities to conduct Expanding Connections seminars. There she "tries to train health care providers how to address a patient's religious history, how to utilize that information in their treatment, and also how to become more comfortable themselves in talking to patients about religion and spirituality. Sometimes that means discovering the workers' own religious past, which might get in the way of their work."

At the end of one of those presentations, a forty-year-old woman on the staff of a mental health facility came to Nancy in tears. "I hadn't ever realized why I quit the church," the woman told her. She explained that her mother died when she was thirteen and at the funeral the priest said everything that happens is God's will. "I couldn't bear that idea," the woman said, "and I stopped going to church. But only now—and it's twenty-five years later—do I see why I stopped. It was because I was angry at the priest!" Though Nancy doesn't know whether the revelation allowed the woman to return to the church, she says that it at least allowed her to feel at peace with why she had left it.

Seeking religious converts is not the goal of her consultation work. Rather, she is practicing her belief that if the areas of religion or spirituality in a patient's life are omitted, important information that can help a worker clinically may be overlooked. "Those areas can be a source of conflict or pain or even a source of help," she says. "Either way, they require that attention be paid."

While she offers these seminars to mental health practitioners, she also conducts pro bono groups with seriously ill mental patients in a psychiatric day treatment program in Cambridge. "These groups are meant to be therapeutic—people have a chance to talk in depth about their religious beliefs. One woman says that she grew up with the idea of a harsh, punitive God, and in the group she has learned to re-think that and come to peace with a different kind of God."

What characterizes Nancy's work in the day treatment program is that while being the leader, she has turned into participant as well. "In the beginning of these groups I went in as just the leader, but over time as I've listened to members of the group talk about their own struggles and the way they find hope and keep going, I sort of internally became more one of them. I don't pretend that I have the answers. I let myself be questioned by their questions to themselves. They've challenged a lot my beliefs, but they've made it clear what a gift I am to them."

She earned the nickname of "the honorary mental patient" and out of the sessions is coming a book in which Nancy hopes to show that even though people have an illness, they still can have questions shared by everyone and spiritual soundness as well.

◆   ◆   ◆

On a 1995 airplane ride from Washington back to Boston, Nancy happened to be seated next to the dean of education at Harvard Medical School. From that serendipitous encounter, plus a few meetings with the dean that Nancy initiated later, came a teaching assignment that she has shared for several years with Ed Lowenstein, a distinguished anesthesiologist. She and Dr. Lowenstein hold a seminar for half a year with a group of eight to ten Harvard medical students. These are third-year students who are just getting past pure theory, going outside the classroom setting for the first time. The idea of the class is to give an opportunity for those future doctors to process what's going on as they have their first practical encounters with the medical world, not in classes but in hospitals.

In their group, says Nancy, the students find a refuge to achieve distance from work in the wards, a place to talk about their experiences, good and bad, mistakes they may see being made in the hospital, even just being treated like the lowest person on the totem pole. "In short," she says, "whatever they want to bring up. Sometimes the discussion simply focuses on what decisions students need to make in their own lives as physicians so that they don't become something negative that they see in others."

As their seminar proceeds, Nancy and Dr. Lowenstein attempt to let the students assume increased responsibility. "Each week there's a different student facilitator, and, after the first session or so, Ed and I act mostly as guides—Ed from a medical point of view and I from a psychological perspective."

With a look of satisfaction, Nancy adds, "I love working with young people, so I really enjoy being with the medical students. And I seem to bring them something as a non-M.D. which they value and which I wouldn't even have expected. I'm glad that Harvard offers this opportunity for future doctors. Medicine tends to be such an isolating field. It's a challenging, sometimes intimidating period these young people are going through, and the seminar is a safe house where they can share experiences with others like them. It's an environment that's nurturing without being touchy-feely.

◆   ◆   ◆

Nancy has never drifted from her religious order, has held several responsible positions and turned down the possibility of others. On four occasions, she was nominated for the post of Provincial or head of all nuns in her order nationwide. One of those times, in 1992, she convened a group of friends to help her decide whether to run for the position or not. (Her motto was to be: "Pray, and party" though she confesses that she slipped and it came out, "Play, and party.") The consensus reached by her friends was that the job would mean an end to all her other work and the contributions she was making to her field. All the same, for a dozen years she acted as liaison between ten local communities and the religious order's central government in St. Louis.

◆   ◆   ◆

"We are six in the community house in Cambridge," Nancy explains, "and we divide up the household responsibilities. Another person and I take turns doing the food shopping, and we all cook on different nights. I like to have a lovely home, so I do the floral arrangements and try to beautify the house." The religious order pays for the community house, and all the income earned by the nuns in their various jobs is sent to the order's central office. The nuns submit a budget for living expenses—food, cars, clothing, and general necessities—and the central office remits to them a monthly check.

"It's easy to kid yourself about what you think is going on with you spiritually, so it's a help to have someone to talk to about that," says Nancy. "I have a mentor, a Franciscan nun, whom I see about once a month to talk about my spiritual life. I've always had somebody like that, somebody I could use as a guide.

"What takes a toll on my own emotional health is being overworked without enough solitary time". She has programmed one escape in the form of a regular Monday afternoon date for tea with a woman psychiatrist friend who lives in nearby Belmont. "It's a valuable time for me, and good therapy for both of us," says Nancy, who offers herself as occasional helper at birthday parties for her friend's young daughter.

Asked whether there were moments when Nancy found her life so difficult that she thought she couldn't continue as a nun, she said yes and singled out one in particular. "In 1978 I had gone to Rome to work on planning a renewal program that my order was going to put on. I'd been working especially hard, was really exhausted, and facing clients in my private practice who were enraged that I was going to be away for six weeks. In fact one of them made a suicide attempt a couple of hours before I was getting on the plane." In Rome, Nancy says that she stood at the top of the Spanish steps thinking that maybe Freud was right, that all this was just an illusion. "When I told that to one of the sisters, she said that what I ought to do is ask God for more faith. And that's what I did."

"I think the key for me is prayer," Nancy concludes. "The times when I don't give enough time to prayer are the times when I see this life as more of a struggle." Though Nancy's everyday work is not church-centered, she attends mass a couple of times a week at a parish in Cambridge and, as a Eucharist minister, she gives out communion during mass.

Nancy works also to incorporate prayer and spirituality into her own daily life, an effort that gives her sustenance. At her 2004 Christmas dinner, for instance—the one she hosted when the community members were away and her guests were mostly not Catholic—she placed small candles by each plate of the ten guests. Before beginning the meal, she asked her friends to light the nearest candle and express whatever feeling of gratitude was in their hearts. "I believe in saying grace before meals, but this was a group of varied religious denominations," she explains. "Asking everyone to express gratitude was my attempt to adapt for them the idea of saying grace." It had an evident mellowing effect on those present. The gratitude that Nancy expressed was for everyone around the table and all the ways they had brought life to her. Her friends seemed to feel that she had done the same for them.

In addition to close friends, family remains an important part of Nancy's life. With the passing of her mother, she has maintained close ties with her brothers and their children. The daughter of one of her brothers is very devout but, according to Nancy, unlikely to consider joining a religious order. "For the most part, women today don't see religious life as an attractive option, because they have a lot of alternatives we didn't have forty years ago. You can be a religious person and very involved and still be out in the world, not taking vows in a religious order."

In a sense, Nancy contradicts this statement, being both in a religious order and well out in the world. She has profited for years from the church's permission for some nuns to eschew the monastic life, sharing that benefit with many around her. In this book about people living alone, Nancy stands out as a person who, though not partnered, is far from alone.

As a woman with earned respect in community and church, she points out that women hold positions as ministers in several other denominations and adds,

"I would love to see women priests, mostly because they have a lot of gifts to bring that are excluded by the laws of the church."

◆   ◆   ◆

As they visit over Monday afternoon tea, Nancy and her friend often do watercolors. Thinking of that, the psychiatrist friend says, "Whatever Nancy starts out painting, a landscape or fruit, it always ends up looking like fireworks are going off. I don't think that's a coincidence."

Raising Young Children While Divorcing: Greg Garland

Until the beginning of 2004, Greg Garland, a mid-forties mechanical engineer, was not only the father of two daughters, Taylor and Rachel, then ages six and four, he was also husband to the children's mother, a Vietnamese woman who had arrived in this country with her family when she was ten. "Our partnership was faltering for some time," says Greg, "enough that we had undertaken four years of marriage counseling. But that January my wife served a restraining order on me. It came as an awful shock—this is no battered-wife story, nothing like that. It's just the way she decided to end the marriage, initiating divorce proceedings with claims of abuse."

The restraining order, he says, jolted Greg back to his time as a student in a class of Shakespeare at Louisiana State University in the 1980s. "Dr. Josephine Roberts taught the course," he recalls. "I was attending engineering school and was the only non-literature student there. One of the things I remember best is Hamlet's phrase, 'Readiness is all,' a phrase that spoke to me in my own life. I plan for rational contingencies but am unprepared when unlikely or irrational events impact my life. That's what happened with my wife's surprise divorce strategy."

Understanding that there are likely two sides to the story, what follows is how, prepared or not, Greg faced an action taken by someone else that profoundly affected him. Determined to remain a good father, he sought a way to continue helping to raise his two small children even though they were all together only part of the time. The family was living in Stamford, a Connecticut suburb about forty miles northeast of New York City. Greg remained in Stamford and moved to a modest apartment that he furnished in a way to host Taylor and Rachel on what later became a fifty-fifty parenting plan. It's not a stylish bachelor pad; rather, one that is kid friendly, with his kids' art the predominant theme on the walls.

To emphasize safety and comfort, Greg gave his new apartment its own name: The Clubhouse. He explains: "I first had extremely limited visitation rights with the girls, then I appealed for and was granted fifty percent custody. I needed a way to explain the arrangement in terms that would make sense to two innocent children—*and* me, for that matter, and still be truthful. I didn't want to lie or create any false hope that the arrangement was just temporary, that Mommy and Daddy would get together again one day, because that could now never happen."

Instead of calling it "Dad's home," Greg told his daughters that the apartment was *our* Clubhouse, meaning a place where they could be free to express themselves without fear and to know love without conditions. "I used palm trees as a decorating motif, telling Taylor that palm trees mark the location of an oasis, a place where a person can get fresh water and be safely restored after a long journey through the desert. She got the idea.

"We posted a sign with our names on it and the names of people we've had over as guests who are Clubhouse members now. One day, when Rachel turned five, she asked if she could put a mommy's name on the list. Yikes! I held my breath and stuttered, 'Well, sure, you can put anyone's name on the list that you want.' 'OK,' she said, 'I'll put Amanda's mommy on the list.' I breathed a sigh of relief that it was somebody else's mom! After months in divorce court, my ex-wife's name is not on the list."

Greg says he didn't call the Clubhouse "Daddy's home" because he wanted Taylor and Rachel to understand that it was not where Daddy chose to live nor the place where he intended to live forever. "My next address won't be the Clubhouse," he says. "We'll simply call it Home."

Greg's children come to stay with him Mondays, Tuesdays, and alternate weekends, yet with all his efforts to make them "Clubhouse safe," Greg says he knows they have sensed something wrong. He has bought books to help make divorce something they can comprehend and, he hopes, not feel blamed for. "Though I still quietly worry, I strive so that as adults they won't have limiting fears of close relationships or of abandonment." Greg also governs his conduct by a stricter standard than that suggested by the courts: whether his children, imagined in adulthood, would approve of his actions. "I try to satisfy the likely adult versions of my kids, which takes violence and abusive behavior off the menu. When I'm talking to my ex-wife, which happens infrequently, it's clinical—information exchange only."

Stamford, Greg says, is the place where he will stay and where he has had to balance fatherhood with caring for his own needs. "I actually wouldn't recommend single parenthood to anybody who is career focused," he says. "Besides being unfair to the child, the person who tries to do both better have a lot of money because he or she will be hiring out a lot of things. Eventually—and it was through the church—I found a wonderful woman named Marlene to come and care for the kids, but in those first months, from January until May, I had no help on that front and no family nearby. Doing everything is a daunting task for one person, and even with a lot of physical and emotional stamina, I was worn down.

"There have been a few times when I stopped to imagine walking away from my responsibilities, to do whatever pleased me. But I am devoted to my kids and they renew me. I could never part from them and still feel whole. I'll always be proud of them for how they've handled this difficult period."

Greg's new locale in Stamford is near Long Island Sound, but, he says, "Connecticut, unfortunately, is no beach getaway for me; it's now a battleground that I did not choose for myself." His battles were mostly with the Connecticut family courts in the months since his divorce proceedings began, a period that he says has been contentious, sometimes exasperating, and always expensive. "As long as my ex-wife could dream up new, unsubstantiated claims," says Greg, "her lawyer was apparently happy to upset any calm I could create for myself and my daughters."

Pleading for recognition as the father has been part of his experience. "After my wife served the divorce papers, I went to both my kids' schools and said I was concerned about their ability to deal with the divorce and wanted to be called if any problem arose. There are counselors in the school that Taylor, the older girl, attends, and I was told that, if necessary, I'd be notified. Twice more I went back to see how she was doing and then in May, just by accident, I learned that my wife had secretly signed her up to see the counselor two weeks before our separation. I was in the school five or six times a week for pick ups and drop offs but never was introduced to the counselor nor did she ask to talk to me. The school at first seemed not to find anything wrong with that! Months later, the principal offered an apology to me in front of my wife."

"Why," asks Greg with exasperation, "does everyone fall into this prejudice that all is fine so long as the mother knows what's going on in a kid's life? Of course, thinks the system, she's the primary custody person. She's a *she!*

"I am interested in telling my story in the hope that others can avoid a calamity like the one foisted upon me. Most people don't know or don't want to know that the system is deliberately made so difficult for fathers. Divorce is a major cause of depression and suicide among men nationally. My situation may be extreme or it may be the norm. All I know is that my life changed radically without my consent at the hands of my ex-wife and significantly enabled by the courts without due process." With a deep breath, he adds, "The law is supposed to protect the weak from the strong, but it is shameful what passes for justice in Connecticut family court."

◆   ◆   ◆

Greg and his wife were both strong people striving to make a worthwhile life, he says, and that was what first attracted them to each other. When they met in 1993, she had gone through public school and earned an engineering degree in Michigan. Over the years, particularly after the birth of their first child, Greg saw that his wife's strengths came from having left a war-torn country to come to America as a young girl with no knowledge of English. "When we faced problems it seemed as if we kept falling back on the same couple of issues, one being her childhood, the other being money," Greg says. "Our first years together were easier financially. We had two pay checks and we paid for our wedding ourselves because her family didn't have the means to do it, but we paid for a lot of it on credit cards, which we shouldn't have done. We weren't careful, and while we had the chance to get ourselves into a financially healthy spot for the future, we wasted it."

Greg says that later, because of consulting work, he was out of town most of the week, and his wife took over paying the bills. Even as he kept getting raises, it seemed as if they never had enough money. One day she told him that they would have to finance paying their taxes for 2001. "I was flabbergasted," he says. "We had kids, a mortgage, and were now deep in debt!"

The other issue, Greg says, perhaps a more deep-seated one, is that his wife's early years were kept closed to him, either willfully or because she was unable to remember them. Her family and her past were taboo. "We did an exercise before we were married which asked a series of questions, beginning with the simplest: 'What was your favorite food as a child?' She said she couldn't remember. And that was her answer to anything to do with her childhood. Any question about how she was raised or her family environment was met with 'I don't know' or 'I don't remember.'

"Eventually I saw that as a red flag that I was sorry not to have noticed sooner. It seems that my wife had developed a perfect version of her life that she wasn't going to have probed into by someone like her husband or even our marriage counselor. Maybe her early years were so traumatic she couldn't remember them or, the counselor suggested after four years of sessions, maybe the trauma that would explain her behavior was just imagined. Regardless, life for me was the same every day. Questions about her past were never answered, an open sharing was never achieved, and I believe this was blocking any chance for our marriage to succeed. My advice to others: Trust but Codify, that is, sign a prenuptial agreement no matter what anyone says."

As for his own situation, he says, "My wife told people that the marriage was failing because I was angry. It's a familiar model: the angry male. Unfortunately, it's a self-fulfilling prophecy that's easier for the public to accept than everything else behind it."

◆   ◆   ◆

Greg spent his early years in California and Louisiana and, later, Texas, whose hundred-degree-plus heat he eventually escaped by going north. With his mechanical engineering background, he moved to New Haven in 1987 for a job "to do high-tech laser stuff." He earned his MBA., met his future wife, and relocated to Stamford in1994, where he has remained on call as a subcontractor to a manufacturer.

Greg grew up the second of four children in a close-knit Catholic family. His father's engineering profession caused them to make moves around the country and occasionally to Western Europe. Today the Garland parents and offspring are spread out on both coasts and parts in between; the only family member living near Greg is his brother Arch, one year younger and in Manhattan.

When their father's seventieth birthday was approaching, Greg says, "Somehow, even though we're all over the map, Arch and Jim, our older brother, and Jennifer, our sister, and I (but mostly they) managed to organize a birthday bash. My contribution was to nail down a place for the event in Pittsburgh, where Mom and Dad have big family connections. It was in 2004, and the party was a wonderful evening with seventy-five people for dinner, singing, speeches, even a barbershop quartet. I attended with my children, without my wife.

"In our family, seventy doesn't mean anything. Dad retired from full-time work but was too energetic to sit and do nothing. Same for Mom. They decided for their next project to own and operate a bed and breakfast. Hiring an architect to design it, they built a Tuscany-style villa on a hilly piece of land they'd found outside Nashville (where, by the way, they'd never lived before). My brother Arch, a graphic designer, created a Web site for them and they started running Sumner's View, a beautifully furnished bed and breakfast in 1999. Dad was already sixty-five."

Upon Greg's divorce, his family grew closer and his parents assumed greater importance. "The divorce got started in January 2004, and my cell phone bill in

February was over five hundred dollars," he recalls. "I would call my folks at any hour, tell them where I was emotionally, physically, spiritually, and they were always supportive. I exchanged e-mails with Mom or Dad or sometimes both, and when I needed a lift, I could read their notes over again. Their advice was to trust in God, remain calm, let the thing go through its cycles, and take care of myself and the girls."

Greg's siblings and friends were on the support team, too. "I have my brothers and sister and a few key individuals who have really helped me stay sane. A couple of friends have taunted me by saying they're 'glad' it's me this is happening to and not someone else, because most other people would have snapped or surrendered already."

To avoid snapping, Greg says, he turned to the church. As a young adult, he saw the church as the world's biggest bank, not as a spiritual leader in his life. "But," he says, referring to the onset of his divorce, "I was hurt and angry and forced to make a choice, either act out negatively, maybe self-destructively, or channel it into some place equipped to handle the strain. Surprisingly to me, religious faith—the church—became my salvation.

"There I was betrayed by my wife and my government and in dire straits emotionally, looking for something I could depend on. What I needed, I realized, was to go way back to lessons I was taught as a child: to believe in a loving God whose plan remains beyond my comprehension. Since my separation, the church has provided me with comfort, just as it has millions of people before me through situations much harder than mine. I now know that God is ready for me to give up some of my burdens. I have seen too many things fall perfectly into place not to now believe that there really is a reason for everything.

"During the regular mass, I heard readings that applied directly to what I was feeling and needed to hear, as if they were talking specifically to me. I sat amazed once when the priest read a passage that ended, 'for whom the Lord loves, he disciplines. He scourges every son he acknowledges.' Imagine how strangely I felt: joyful that God cared enough to smite me personally. It was then that I remembered how to laugh at myself and my predicament, and it was then that things began to get much better.

"A friend of mine talks about being a 'recovering Catholic.' Maybe that's what I was…or just desperate. But for a couple of months the church was all I had to lean on. I remain grateful that it was there for me."

How Greg will raise his daughters remains to be seen. "My wife, who previously had no religious history, has already rejected the Catholic faith. That item I leave on God's plate."

◆   ◆   ◆

When Greg has free time, which he says was curtailed once the divorce got underway, he swims, and that, together with biking, makes him an amateur candidate for triathlons, in which he participates on an occasional Sunday. He is, by reputation, an accomplished cook, and a future objective is to resume instruction to earn his private pilot's license, a goal set years ago. Plus, he wants to build his existing business to the point where he is able to work when he wants to work, retire when he wants to, and take care of himself and his daughters through college. "For graduate school, they'll be on their own financially but fully supported in all other parental ways, just as I was."

Greg's retired-but-not-retired father isn't the only one in the family with a full tank of energy. The person who created the Type A designation had his eyes on Greg. "I'm at my happiest," he says, "when I'm facing a challenge and making some headway. That might be at 1 or 2 AM. It's after 11 PM that I'm at my most creative and constructive. Let's call it undiagnosed insomnia or a critical success enabler. I believe that I need less sleep than normal. Eight hours or more makes me groggy." Greg's norm is to get to bed at or after 1 AM and wake up around six hours later. With only six hours of sleep, he can begin each day with a huge lead.

Was this late-night work habit a problem while married, he is asked? Greg says that yes, bedtime hours were different for him and his wife, but even if they had worked out that issue, it wouldn't have resolved the fundamental problems that remained.

If you're on Greg's e-mail list, you're likely to receive a message that he created after most others have packed it up for the day. One time, he wrote, "It is now 1:17 AM and I'm just getting comfortable at the keyboard." No less improbably, the message might have been sent off in a restless flurry at 7 AM. "Tonight," he wrote at 2:30 AM, "I WENT OUT INTO the wasteland that is Connecticut's live music scene. I found but one place that had a groove and knew what it was for. All other taverns think that providing beer in clear glasses is ample 'entertainment.' Having grown up in New Orleans, I prefer live music." An afterthought to this message read, "Last night I didn't get to sleep until 3:30. Tonight I must sleep ASAP and it is now 1:30. Usually, my fatigue goes undetected by others, but I know it impairs my enjoyment of subsequent days, if nothing else."

Greg believes his habit of late night work is fueled by the stamina resulting from conditioning for triathlons, but the interlocutor suspects an avoidance of post-midnight loneliness. Is it? "Maybe," Greg replies, though he claims not to typically think in such terms since, he says, "that term—loneliness—is loaded with victim-hood." Solitude is the term that he prefers, as it implies choice. "I see the available time as freedom—though if the right woman were to appear, truth be told, I would gladly abandon my keyboard or reserve that book on my night stand for another evening."

◆   ◆   ◆

The long-range question of whether Greg foresees remaining single, without a partner, seems not a concern at the moment. "I'm presuming that I'm going to be a single parent for a good many years," he says. "If I go out on a date, it's not to search for a bride." What predominates his thinking now are ensuring his own growth and the growth and well-being of young daughters, and granting himself an occasional night out with friends.

Early on in my meetings with Greg, he claimed that the single life was over-rated. "I can go out for several hours and have a great time with friends, old and new," he said, "only to have it neutralized by a twenty-minute drive home that is lonely and sad." Not banishing the possibility of an opposing point of view, Greg added, "I suspect that for me, living happily but alone was inevitable, given my personality. When I date, and I do at times, I enjoy the time, but from what I have learned about family law in twenty-first century America, my lifestyle is likely to stay as it is for a good while."

Though it was an unwished-for jolt when his wife filed for divorce, Greg reflects, "Only months later did I find out how much I prefer it to being married to an unhealthy person. When she pushed me away, I needed a while to recognize the magnitude of the gift she unknowingly gave me. My life had been about duty, trying to make the marriage work for all four of us. Doing the impossible has now been lifted from my plate, and there's a tremendous relief. My new life is far better than digging in and surviving the storm, which it was for years. I can create and attain my own dreams without my wife's negativity. I've taken the time to surround myself with healthier people. Freedom, I believe, is the very foundation of happiness."

Does there then remain a contradiction between Greg's finding the single life over-rated but believing he may have been destined to live alone? The answer seems that he is willing to accept both as possibilities. "It is up to me if I wish to interpret living without a partner as 'bad.' The fact that companionship is infrequent doesn't mean that I must now be living a sub-quality life."

Even as he works to be a fair-minded adult and parent, Greg appears struggling to deal with the emotions that can run high throughout a difficult divorce process. The same may be true for his wife. Still short of the half-century mark, Greg looks well into the future and says, "I don't expect my days to be pure happiness. In fact, happiness is not a goal. Overall, I'm living a good life. When my friends seem as if they're worried about unimportant, trivial things, I look squarely at them and say, 'Listen, there are six billion people living on this planet, and almost all of them wish they had your life.' I remind myself of that often.

"My previous life was filled with futility because I was trying too hard to make someone else happy. I think we do have considerable say over how we respond to the challenges in our lives, and my plan now is to think and act in ways to benefit my children and myself. Yes, I still feel sad sometimes, and that's OK. I wish I felt it less often and that's OK, too."

◆   ◆   ◆

Arch, Greg's closest brother in age and one with whom he shared a room growing up, says, "Even as a kid, Greg approached life with an engaging spirit. It doesn't surprise me that he has become überfather. He loves his kids' company, and vice-versa. Greg is a genuinely curious listener who explains things to his little girls with a gentle warmth."

Post script: In Fall 2005 Greg's divorce case was settled in Connecticut Family Court. Greg retains half (fifty per cent) custody of his daughters. Without full legal custody, his ex-wife is prevented from moving out of the jurisdiction without the judge's approval, unlikely unless Greg seeks the same destination for himself and their children. Greg has no obligation to pay alimony or child support because he and his ex-wife are earning comparable salaries. He signs away the deed to the family's house, retaining just enough cash to pay off the family's collective back taxes.

After the long divorce case, Greg says that all is well and getting better all the time.

Choosing Independence Above Income: Susan E. Davis

Susan Davis's first work as a young graduate of Mt. Holyoke College in 1964 was as a trainee in a New York City publishing firm. From there she went to an editor's desk, but it was a job that ended after just six years when she was fired, in the official version, for "terrorism, obscenity, and interfering with the authority of a superior." Susan's explanation was that she was dismissed for trying to organize a union in the company. Looking back thirty-five years later, her attempt at unionizing seems to have been an offshoot to a beginning involvement in progressive political causes. They have added up to countless demonstrations and six arrests for civil disobedience.

Susan moved from the publishing house in the early 1970s to a four-year unpaid stint editing an alternative women's magazine while doing political work and living with a man in Brooklyn. With that period over, she rented an apartment in Chelsea, a Manhattan neighborhood then considered off the beaten path, now trendy and expensive. To work on design books, she went to the Whitney Library of Design as a book production editor. But, of that job Susan says, "After awhile, I got so bored with book production, and I wanted to do my own writing, be my own boss." She left the Whitney Library in 1984 and began to build a freelance career by writing in part about graphic design, her acquired specialty.

In the last two decades, Susan has managed, she might say scraped by, with several "full-time, part-time" jobs. "Even if it's a challenge financially, and it is, I love being on my own," she says. "It fits my need to have my own space and time, and I certainly don't miss the pressure to conform. That was particularly strong in the late 1970s and early '80s when I was 'out' as a lesbian and the only one in the office. I felt very alone. It may be different today, but the atmosphere was far from accepting at that time, even in New York City, even in a reputedly liberal profession like publishing."

People who depend for their livelihood on freelancing know very well about the tradeoff. While you relish being your own boss, it's you who has to pull in work to pay the bills. Had she remained in corporate publishing, Susan likely would be earning a handsome income. Working for herself for twenty years, she has depended on a succession of jobs and, as she points out, "when there's a dry spell or when a job falls through, income evaporates and times grow lean." It's large book projects or long-term journalism assignments that have helped her to survive, including one that came her way in 2004 when a retiring editor recommended her to write a monthly newsletter for architects and engineers. "Though the articles cover business topics that aren't the most exciting, the writing is challenging, especially because I've got to meet a strict deadline," she says.

That newsletter job continues to provide work, but it doesn't prevent money from remaining a constant issue. "I have one thing on my side," Susan says, "and that's the rent protection that New York City laws grant to people who stay in the same apartment for years (or decades, in her case)." On the other hand, there are things she says that she has had to skip that she'd like to have done…"and," she adds, "I'll admit that I'm wildly in debt."

But she has felt no pull to return to full-time publishing. "No," Susan adds with a grin, "there's never been an urge to go back to a publishing company. I've got to be my own boss, and even when times are lean, I manage to indulge in *some* things that for me are necessities—the occasional bunch of eucalyptus leaves or tickets for dance and theater and opera performances. I *have* to go to the Met even if it means sitting at the top."

When income-producing work or political work doesn't interfere—and that isn't often—Susan moves ahead on the third version of a book she began writing in 1979. "I love any kind of writing, but when I'm doing my novel I feel most authentically myself," she says. "The plot takes on abortion head on." Susan has published four non-fiction books along with numerous articles for the graphic design press.

Susan's work on the novel led her to join the National Writers Union, an organization of some 3,500 writers spread around the country. Characteristically, she became involved, first being elected co-chair of the New York chapter in 2000 and, in 2004, as second vice president of the national organization. It's a close cousin to her political work. "Publishers have run all kinds of scams to not pay writers what they deserve, to withhold reprint rights, sometimes not to pay for work at all," she states angrily. "These are perhaps the most important issues the union addresses." Beyond that, the union tries to develop programs to help writers write and to increase visibility of writers' issues. "Like any good union, we provide a place where members can voice their concerns as a group and take action to defend their rights. We are their advocates."

For the past six years Susan has also attended a week-long conference of the International Women's Writing Guild. "It's a gathering of three to four hundred women all focusing on different aspects of writing, and it creates an incredible sense of community and bonding. You can bring writing, you can sell books, and you can write while attending the workshops. There you get immediate feedback on what you've done, and that is very therapeutic. Women recognize that the struggle to get published is very real, that others are going through the same struggle that you are going through. It's really supportive."

◆   ◆   ◆

Susan is now in her early sixties, and over these decades that she has occupied the same studio apartment in Chelsea, hers has remained the only uninterrupted name on the mailbox downstairs. She hasn't always been alone upstairs; although her lodgings are typically New York single-person modest, she has shared them with partners who have rotated between men and women and men again. But none have evolved into marriage. "I've had numerous romantic relationships," says Susan, "but I haven't chosen to settle for one that's mediocre just to be married."

Being a freelance writer who does her work at home, Susan says that she needs space and time alone to nurture her creativity and that she likes living by herself. Actually, there is a roommate whose name hasn't made it to the mailbox: a one-eyed cat named Jack., who also seems happier without a quarrelsome sibling lately transferred to a country life.

Limited quarters turn Manhattanites into masters at making small spaces serve multiple functions as they become warm and inviting along the way. Helped along by her experience on design books, Susan has created an apartment that works for a writer and is stamped with her busy, right-out-there persona. In a roomy kitchen, she added beside the sink and stove a long desk with computer and crowded ceiling-high bookshelves, making the room into kitchen, office, library, and dining area for Jack. Everything else for living in Apartment 4A she has assigned to the one-and-a-half remaining rooms: a convertible futon, conglomeration of more books, still more books, pictures, colorful patterned rugs and covers, and dozens of souvenir posters of left-of-center politics. In her casual layered clothes, Susan fits the prototype of a female political activist—assertive voice, full figure, and round face topped by a head of short, spiky snow-white hair.

Through the start and finish of those male and female romantic attachments, Susan's unwavering attachment has been with various progressive causes and the promotion of peace that she traces back to high school. In her native Rochester, New York, she was president of the junior council of the local association for the United Nations. "It gave me a consciousness about politics and the world," she says. That continued in college and all the years beyond, with a resume today that includes attendance at and organization of hundreds of demonstrations over four decades, plus those half-dozen arrests for civil disobedience that go back to one in the late 1960s during a protest against racism. She also organized and led major demonstrations for abortion and reproduction rights in New York City between 1977 and 1992.

Susan's route into progressive politics has a connection to her family background, but not because her parents were staunchly liberal. It's, in a roundabout way, because while studying to be an Episcopalian minister, her father realized that what he truly sought was something different—one world religion. That led him in 1932 to forsake the Episcopal Church and become a Bahai (defined by Webster as "a religion founded in Iran and teaching the essential worth of all races and religions and equality of the sexes"). "But," Susan explains, "there weren't many Bahais in the United States, so when it came time for my brother and me to receive religious training, my parents decided to send us to the nearby Presbyterian Church.

"One of my earliest memories, when I was eight, was of the minister saying to me, 'I hear your father is a heathen.'" Susan's reaction was to think, "I don't like this man. He doesn't know my father, my father is a good person." That experience and others turned her eventually against that church, so at age eleven, when either she or her parents had to join the congregation, her mother yanked both Susan and her brother away from the Presbyterians and moved them to the Unitarian Church.

"When I was about sixteen I went with my parents to a Bahai summer school in Maine. I discovered how much that faith appealed to me. There is no clergy, and it leaves it up to you to individually establish your own relationship with God and the world around you. I especially loved the emphasis on world peace, the abolition of every kind of prejudice, and the equality between men and women. Though I had liked being a Unitarian, at eighteen I took a big step and decided also to become a Bahai." Her mother became a Bahai the same year: 1960.

It was in April 1966, during the Vietnam War and a rapidly growing anti-war movement, that Susan remembers going with a friend on her first peace march on

Fifth Avenue in Manhattan. Already devoted to the Bahai faith with its belief in world peace, she says that first taste of a peace movement began her conversion to a determined protestor against the war.

"As time went on and I attended more demonstrations, I became more opposed to the draft," Susan says, "and it soon became clear to me that I had to become a political activist." But she faced an unwished-for incongruity, because one of the precepts of the Bahai world faith is that you must abide by the rules of the state where you live and take no sides politically. "It forced me to make a tough choice, between politics and religion. In 1969, three years after that march on Fifth Avenue, I left the Bahais. Ironically, though, the principles of that faith—equality, world peace, absence of prejudice—provided the foundation for my political life in pursuit of the same ideals."

As long as she remains politically active, Susan is prohibited from rejoining the faith. But the faith resurfaced in her life at least spiritually during her father's illness in the early 1990s. "I traveled regularly to Florida where my parents were living in Ft. Myers, and I spent a lot of time with him. Before he went to sleep, I read him Bahai prayers. It reawakened in me how meaningful they are. After he died and I was left to take care of Mother, I felt overwhelmed and knew that I couldn't do that on my own, so I started saying Bahai prayers myself. I continue to do so daily." Susan calls her religion today "eclectic new-age," made up part from Bahai and part from a variety of other spiritual practices.

Starting in 2001 Susan helped organize several major anti-war marches and rallies, and in 2004 she joined in the April million-plus March for Women's Lives in Washington. "What an encouraging, exciting outpouring of women of all ages and ethnic backgrounds," she says. But those efforts only capped decades of protesting. During a period of six years when she was "out," there were demonstrations for gay rights, plus a continuing string of actions on behalf of women's issues.

With a hint of pride, Susan recalls her record of being arrested, mostly in New York but also in Washington, sometimes in opposition to apartheid in South Africa, more often for demonstrations to do with women's or abortion rights, one of which closed down the Brooklyn Bridge in 1989. Speaking with the experience of a veteran, she says, "When you're arrested with a group of people for civil disobedience around a political issue, there's a special camaraderie. There was one time though, in 1996, when I was arrested by myself—at the dedication of a new statue of Eleanor Roosevelt in Manhattan. I was protesting the cutting of welfare, and I got hauled off to a police precinct on the Upper West Side and was chained for a few hours to a cage. Thank heavens, I'd had the other arrests, so I knew what was going on and that people were going to get me out. But while I was there, four FBI officials interrogated me, and they never returned my finger-prints. I'm sure they're still in a file somewhere in Washington."

These days it is not age but bad knees that put Susan on the sidelines of marches. Still, plenty of less physically-demanding work goes on. In fact, she says she hears from other people, "You're the only person I know who's still politically active. How can you do it?"

Her answer is, "But I have to. It's who I am."

◆   ◆   ◆

Everyone in this book lives without a partner, some having remained unat-tached throughout their adult years, some having exited long-term affairs or mar-riages. Susan is unique here in her history of intimate relationships with both genders. "Though I haven't been with a woman for two decades, I consider myself to be bisexual," she says. "I am still attracted to women and have a large number of very close women friends."

Her time as a lesbian followed years of dating men in relationships that, she says, had left her disappointed. "What made me change was fairly simple—frus-tration with men, followed by meeting a very attractive woman. She and I had a fling, and then I decided I was a lesbian." That "out" period continued for six plus years. According to Susan, it ended when she ran into a man on the street for whom she had had an attraction years earlier. "He was married but emotionally available; one thing led to another, he left his wife, and I was with him for nearly the next five years.

"From today's vantage point, that man was probably the love of my life, but it was an awfully difficult situation. He was at times depressed, at times suicidal, even homicidal. My independence flew out the window; I became needy and subservient and collapsed myself into the relationship, trying to help him. That didn't work, and it didn't help me. We made each other crazy. It was a horrible ending, but out of it I learned that I had to become a self-reliant individual and not depend on a relationship with another person to give me what I didn't have inside. I've been with other men since then, but I've learned now that as soon as I recognize that the relationship isn't going to work, I say goodbye. That is what I have to do."

◆   ◆   ◆

For the last twenty years, Susan says that she has been working on herself, a lot of that time being spent in therapy—and a lot of that to free herself from her parents. "They have been the biggest challenge I've had to overcome. My father was a source of unconditional love for me; we had a spiritual bond plus a physical resemblance. But while he was very passive, my mother was very aggressive, and I believe from the time I was a baby, she was jealous of the relationship between him and me. She was critical and mean and controlling."

Susan says that therapy has helped her move from resistance to open confrontation. "There was a time when I went to Florida to visit at Christmas after my parents had moved from an apartment into a nearby assisted-living facility. It was 1994 and I was trying to put up holiday lights to make their place look cheerier. My mother said nastily, 'Oh, don't bother. There's no point to it.' I said, 'If you don't want me to do it, I won't, but I'm not going to argue with you.' She persisted in picking on me and finally I said, 'Mother, I'm not taking this any more. I'm leaving,' and I walked out and drove back to their old apartment. A few minutes later, Mother called and said, 'I'm sorry, I shouldn't have been so difficult.' My mother had *never* said 'I'm sorry' before. That was really an important moment for me, the first time I openly stood up to her."

When Susan's father died in 1995, and there was no longer someone to be jealous of, Susan says that her mother radically changed. "I continued to visit her in Florida, and once, when she and I were on a vacation together in Cape Cod, I was reading her Bahai prayers and suddenly she said to me, 'Susan, I know I haven't always been the best mother to you, but I want you to know I have always loved you.' After that, her whole way of being became more loving and appreciative. She would thank me for doing things for her, especially as she became more dependent. It was like she had had a personality transplant. We had transformed our relationship by the time she died."

Susan believes that others who have gone through something like this know what an ordeal it is, but that the result is wonderful when the person comes out of it. "I think that having such a difficult mother went a long way to shaping who I am," she says. "I either had to give in to her or stand up to her, and I chose to stand up and rebel. It was the right choice for me."

◆   ◆   ◆

It isn't long in Susan's apartment that the phone remains quiet. Her brother in the Midwest, political and union colleagues, opera friends, miscellaneous pals, and many "sisters" whom she has adopted along the way are frequent callers. If she says that the frustrating part of her life is the lack of time to be alone to devote to her novel, it's not hard to believe. "I wish there were more time for that," she says ruefully, "but one day I'll be ready for the process (ordeal) of getting it published."

Aside from Susan's wished-for times by herself, there are forced times alone, such as a recent Thanksgiving when she was sick at home with pneumonia, maybe caused by overwork. "I had made a turkey meat loaf the night before," she says smiling, "so I there I was at home, eating it and some canned cranberry sauce. It was probably the worst Thanksgiving I've ever had…but it was still OK. Lying in bed, there were times when I felt lonely. But I realized that I could pick up the phone at any point and call my brother and his family in Minnesota or several friends who would be there for me. I'm lucky because Jack, my cat, likes to snuggle. He cuddled up next to me, so I thought, 'Well, maybe I'm not really lonely. Maybe I'm just a little bored because I can't get out.'"

Loneliness, Susan says, permeated her childhood, but now it is mostly foreign to her, perhaps because she's so busy and has worked through a lot in therapy. "I'm lucky in that way, I guess. I used to feel lonely, used to feel there was hurt in my heart. But now when I experience pain or am aware of my needy 'child,' I try to really comfort myself without waiting to be comforted by another person. I just put my hand over my heart…and it helps.

"At this point, in my early sixties, I don't feel single in the way it was defined in the 1940s and '50s. I'm definitely not what used to be called a spinster, and I don't require another person to feel fulfilled. If someone came along now, I wouldn't turn the person down…but I'm not looking. One of my quests is to be as fully realized a human being as I can be, and I think that a crucial element for me is having a peaceful home that's just mine."

"Besides," she jokes, "there aren't many people who want to put up with my lifestyle, anyway."

◆   ◆   ◆

Eleanor Bader, a friend for many years from the women's movement, writes: "Perhaps being single allows Susan to devote herself to her political work and allows her to maintain a more single-minded focus than folks with partners or kids. I am always astounded by her ability to stay positive, and not get mired in depression over how screwed up the world is. She still holds the big picture in her heart and head."

Keeping Travel as Essential as Work: Wayne Hoffman

Wayne Hoffman's mailing address is a studio apartment in Manhattan's Greenwich Village, but you'll find him in residence as infrequently as he can manage. It isn't that he doesn't like New York; it's that he has an unbridled passion for travel. "The bug hit me when I was a small child," Wayne says. "There wasn't a single day that I didn't spend time looking at maps, atlases, or my globe. In fact, that's still true today. I'd read about another place in an encyclopedia, then I'd look for it on a map and imagine what it'd be like to go there." By now, he has converted the imagining into actual visits to a considerable number of those places.

Being still in his mid-thirties, Wayne is too young for retirement, and since he isn't independently rich, he has to create a balance between satisfying the travel itch and paying the rent. Ideally, he says, he would like not to have a full-time job. But he has had several, all to do with writing or editing. They haven't handicapped his urge for getaways, however, to spots as distant as Peru or Ecuador and for as little as a weekend. These trips often are done last minute with inexpensive airfares found on the Internet.

Mark Sullivan, Wayne's close friend, shares his wanderlust and his approach to travel. When they go together, they strive to use transportation that locals take and to avoid anywhere that tourists eat. Wayne says that he and Mark visited the Colosseum in Rome for about ten minutes and then boarded a train to find a village in Umbria where they could see the countryside and dine on cheese. "In Athens," he adds almost apologetically, "we did spend an afternoon at the Acropolis, but the following day we rented a car to go around a random Greek isle—whichever one we could get to on the next ferry. Shared bathrooms are OK, and in the tropics we can cope without hot water. But at this age we need real beds to sleep on."

There came a time in 2002 when Wayne was so unhappy in his work as an editor at *Billboard* magazine (suicidally miserable, he says) that he called his friend, screaming desperation. He found Mark, an editor at *Fodor's*, in a similar state. Sometimes, Wayne says, his friend offers notions for trips that don't hold up in the light of day. This time he threw out his wildest idea to date: a trip through Mexico and all of Central America, nothing hurried, five or six months—long enough that the trip couldn't be made without leave-taking from both their jobs. "Give me a day to think about it," was what Wayne said, and a day was what it took for him to agree.

Once the commitment was made, the two men realized that such a long getaway would be impossible without stashing away funds, which translated into staying at their desks for another six months and taking on freelance assignments as well. "It's what we did," says Wayne. "Then, in August 2002, Mark and I landed in San Antonio, and we went south and didn't come back to New York until the next February."

Managing editors are known for attention to detail, and that's what Wayne addressed before he left on his jaunt. Leaving a job to search for new work is less foolhardy than giving up a New York apartment to search for a replacement, so as first priority he researched the legality of sub-leasing his studio to ensure it would remain his on his return. After securing written landlord approval, Wayne signed his own sub-leasing agreement with a man who stayed while he was gone. (For Mark, leaving town was, he says, a relative cinch, since he'd just lost his apartment.)

That was just the beginning of the list. "I worry a lot about the little things in advance, so once I'm gone, I don't have to worry," says Wayne. "I got my inoculations and international driver's license, made notes for my parents of all my credit cards, had my phone changed to the renter's name and my mail forwarded to my parents' home. I burned CDs so I could have music on the road. I bought a used computer and Mark bought a *second* used computer so it could be sent in case the first one was stolen (which it never was). I made CARE packages for myself and sent them ahead, one to Mexico City, one for later to Costa Rica, and a third for my sister to bring when she came to visit in Guatemala, between the two other places."

The plan that the friends laid out was to follow the Inter-American Highway from the top of Mexico to the rain forest in the bottom of Panama. Says Wayne, "Mark and I thought that traveling the highway would give some shape to the trip and maybe offer the theme for a book later. We rented a car only a few days the entire time; otherwise, we went by bus and stayed for the most part on or close to the highway. If the notion hit, we felt free to change plans on the fly, and we occasionally went separate ways during the day, which was good for both of us. Mark is a lot more interested in exploring ruins than I am. I'd have murdered him if he dragged me to another ancient temple."

Given the challenge of spending six months in one room with any person, Wayne reports that they managed successfully. "In all that time we had separate rooms only once, and that was when we found a pathetically cheap place to stay—four dollars per night—and also because I was sick. We stayed together so much partly because there were times when it would have been dangerous to go out alone, so we *needed* to stay together. We were in places where maybe there weren't restaurants, or where there wasn't anyone else who spoke English. Sometimes we were in a town where there wasn't a town at all."

That wasn't true of their first major stop, Mexico City, a traffic-clogged metropolis of some twenty-four million people, which they reached after a couple of weeks in small villages of northern Mexico. In the Mexican capital they took a month's rental of a one-bedroom apartment. Wayne had lined up a freelance article about Jewish life in Mexico City to be sent to *Hadassah Magazine*. Though he had quit *Fodor's*, Mark was still assigned freelance work for them, also in Mexico.

As they then proceeded south, Wayne says, he kept notes on everything they did, a running travelogue that he sent home once a week. "I wrote enough for a book, but I got distracted and it hasn't been written so far. One night in Chiapas, the southern state of Mexico, when I couldn't sleep, a novel suddenly hit me. I kept trying to doze off, but the story kept coming, characters and plots, too. I got up, went in the bathroom so I could turn on the light without waking up Mark, and I sat in the bathtub with my clothes on and sketched out a novel."

Being a newspaper editor doesn't teach you about writing a novel, and Wayne had never written one. But he says the story wouldn't go away and by the time they got back, he had written four chapters. "That's not a lot," he says, "but I decided to keep on with it and postpone writing about Central America. A year later, I'd finished a novel and had fifty thousand words and a lot of pictures about Central America—but no book."

Wayne had budgeted the entire six months and says that he even came in a little below budget. But the end of the trip wasn't the end of expenses. He returned without an income-producing job. "I hoped nothing would come up for a few months and I'd scrape by and finish my novel, but that's not what happened. I started sending out occasional resumes, answering ads for managing editors. *That* I know how to do! One of the first places I applied was *The Forward*, they called me in and, after a third interview, offered me a job."

What to do? "It was the end of February, and I wasn't really ready to go back to work, but it was a job offer in bad times, and I was running out of money. So I accepted the offer and asked when they wanted me to start. 'Tomorrow,' they said. Mark was traveling again—to Peru this time—so I said, 'You need to give me a week. There's something I have to do.' I went home, got online, bought an airline ticket for the next day, and called Mark in Lima. 'I'm gonna be there tomorrow,' I told him." After that, it was heavy duty, managing the intricacies of publishing *The Forward*'s weekly paper.

◆   ◆   ◆

Because Mark sometimes travels independently of Wayne and sometimes doesn't have his own place, he unloads his luggage in Wayne's 250-square-foot studio when he hits New York. Though Wayne claims that he loves having his friend there ("we cook dinner and watch TV, very domestic"), he terms the arrangement "extraordinarily difficult" since in one room it's hard for either of them to work or talk on the phone when the other person is never more than a few feet away. Besides that, Wayne is a night owl and Mark is up with the sun, so if one light is on, the whole apartment is light.

As one of the youngest persons in this book, sexually active Wayne says that the "extraordinarily difficult" part of Mark's staying with him in New York is sex. "My sex life these days largely involves having men I meet come over. With Mark staying here, I'm without a place to 'entertain.' But what can you do? Mark is family and more important than a trick, even if that's what I really need at the moment."

Unlike some in this book, Wayne does not portray himself as a type destined from childhood to live by himself. "I never set out to intentionally live alone," he says. "I lost a sublet in New York City when I was twenty-four. It was her apartment and her girlfriend wanted to move in, so I had to move out. I didn't want to move into someone else's place for fear I would lose that eventually, too, so I got my own studio to have some sense of security and control over my living arrangements. Only after I moved in did I realize how wonderful it is to live alone."

When he dates, Wayne says, he often realizes that he prefers being single. He has catalogued the advantages. "It's certainly less of a hassle, less stressful, less drama, and easier to plan. I don't have to answer to anyone, don't have to justify what I do or to explain myself." Slightly less unequivocal, he adds, "Of course there are days when it's lonely, but that's true when you're dating, too."

As for physical closeness, he says, "Sometimes I just want someone to sleep in my bed, but I can usually find a man to do that when I need it—at least when I have the place to myself."

Ten years into life in his studio apartment, a friend asks Wayne, "Do you have any regrets today about living alone?"

"There's nobody else to scrub the shower. That's about it."

◆   ◆   ◆

Wayne is a person on whom early years did not go to waste. He grew up in Silver Spring, Maryland, in the house where his parents still reside, and he had his first boyfriend at sixteen, the summer before enrolling in Tufts University in Boston in 1987. He quickly became active in gay organizations and told his parents about his sexuality shortly thereafter. Those, Wayne recalls, were the early days of college melding into an omni-sexual experience. "My first two years I shared a dormitory room with a wonderful straight man, and there were times when his girlfriend would spend the night with him in the top bunk and my boyfriend would spend the night with me in the bottom one. Sort of like the queer Waltons."

Mark Sullivan entered his life when Wayne took off a semester after his sophomore year, and Mark became his lover for the rest of his college career. "I had done writing for my high school and college papers," Wayne says. "In June 1989 I met Mark, an editor at *The Washington Blade*, through a personal ad in that same paper." *The Washington Blade* is one of the principal gay papers in the country. It was shortly after the two met, and at Mark's request, that Wayne wrote a music review for "The Blade," his first piece of professional journalism. "I felt awkward writing for my lover, but when I met the publisher and he commented that he enjoyed my article and hoped I'd continue, I realized it wasn't sheer nepotism." Wayne continued writing pop music reviews and, later, interviews, book reviews, arts coverage, and political columns. "Eventually Mark encouraged me to write a regular feature about media and then to try to syndicate, which I did.

"I moved to New York in 1993 for graduate school at NYU, and when 'The Blade' launched its New York edition in 1997, Mark moved from Washington and wound up at the helm. He contacted me about joining their staff. That meant leaving school, but it was my first chance to become a full-time journalist." With Mark training him, Wayne came on as the paper's arts editor. In the years since he met Mark, he says that he has written for perhaps two hundred editors. "But Mark is still the best, by far."

◆   ◆   ◆

Although Wayne has stayed in New York and his parents have remained in Maryland, neither distance nor religious differences have prevented them from maintaining a close relationship. "I used to call my parents a couple of times a week," Wayne says. "About five years ago my mother had an extremely difficult time, so I started calling her every day from work, to check on how she was. That continues today."

Wayne's parents keep a Kosher home as he did also through his teen years. He says that he never brings non-Kosher food into their house. His brother, seven years older, is a rabbi, married with children, living on Long Island. "Actually," Wayne suggests with a grin, "when my folks come to New York, they prefer to stay with me—in my tiny apartment—instead of Long Island with my brother and his wife and three boys. It's quieter here."

Time strengthened the family ties, but those ties did not prevent Wayne from becoming a self-described Jewish atheist. "As I was growing up, I went through the traditional stuff: trips to Israel, Bar Mitzvah, and attendance at a Labor Zionist youth camp. But as soon as there was an option and one could stop the usual progression—it was after my Bar Mitzvah—I told my parents that I wasn't going to go on any further with Hebrew school. They, of course, were not happy at all. My brother had been confirmed, my sister also. But by then I had decided that I not only didn't happen to believe, I actively didn't believe in God."

He did not terminate religious education for a lack of interest in Judaism. It interests him still, he says, the culture and politics particularly. "My brother and sister had been in the National Bible Contest, my brother went to the international finals in Israel twice, my sister got to the national. I loved reading and studying the Bible, so I entered the Bible Contest, too. In fact, when our teacher left—I was thirteen—I said, 'I'll teach it.' I no longer attended Hebrew school, but I took on students at home and stayed a contestant myself."

Today, Wayne observes those Jewish holidays that don't require attendance at the synagogue. "What's the point of going to synagogue and not praying?" he asks. Instead, he prepares latkes for Chanukah, hamantashen for Purim—and with his dark beard and vaguely rabbinical look he goes for Passover back to his parents' home (no paradox noted) to conduct his family's Seder. "We've shared Passover with another family for years," he says, "and for us it's something of a party. I run it as a sort of gay/socialist/atheist Seder, extraordinarily irreverent. We sing the same songs everyone else sings, only with a sense of humor. My brother's not there—he's busy on holidays, so it's my show. If he were there, he'd probably do more of the Hebrew that I skip, but…I love Passover!" (Being nearly a part of the family, Mark goes to the Hoffman's for Passover too.)

Wayne does more than telephone and share Passover with his parents. Along with Mark Sullivan, they've become traveling companions of his. "We've been to Paris and Venice and Brussels together, and I try to be sure that we see Jewish landmarks, especially in less likely places like Mexico City, where they came when I was living there. We used a guide to show us Jewish areas I'd never have found on my own. My folks are nervous about things like language, directions, food, but they're easy for me, so when we go together I make the plans and they can relax. Sometimes I arrive a day or two in advance to scope out the place."

In early 2005 Wayne led a Hoffman family journey to Costa Rica, a trip that included Mark and Wayne's sister, four years his senior, a veterinarian who lives in Phoenix and shares his taste in music. "Costa Rica is a country my parents would never have visited unless I took them," says Wayne.

Looking back to his time of growing up, he adds, "My parents were fairly permissive with me, so it seems as if I simply never had much to rebel against. I was never a bad kid. I think the worst thing I ever did was to come home an hour after curfew—once! I made sure they knew about my being gay early on. As for religion, I've never disrespected their devotion to Judaism. My ties to it are different from theirs and I think they understand that.

"We're a strange family. We all really like each other."

Is there a benefit that Wayne derives from this closeness with his mother and father?

"I guess I never thought of the benefit," he says. "I always thought of the downside of not doing it—I wouldn't be as close to them as I am. I love my parents!"

◆   ◆   ◆

A friend inquired whether it bothered Wayne that in his mid-thirties he doesn't seem to have mapped out a conventional kind of career. "I always wanted to be a writer and a teacher," he says. "The question was whether I'd be a writer who taught on the side or a teacher who wrote on the side. I'd really like not to have a full-time job, but then how do you pay for a place to live, and what do you do about health insurance?"

Practical though he is, Wayne says that he doesn't want to emulate his father, whom he describes as very much a workaholic, a man who takes a dictating machine when he goes to the beach. "That's not for me. I think of a job as what you do to make the money to have the life you want." The job at *The Forward*, he says, doesn't make him want to kill himself, so it's a step up. But he notes that he doesn't see any job as permanent, since full-time office work keeps him from writing and traveling as much as he would like. "It fills me with ennui and is dissatisfying on almost every level."

Wayne reports having met older men who managed successfully with never having had a full-time job, but even those men say that it's probably impossible today because New York is too expensive. "As soon as I moved to Greenwich Village, I realized that I'd discovered the place where I'm meant to live. I'm very happy that I found somewhere that feels like home. But I can't really make the numbers crunch, so I sacrifice by having a full-time job that makes me crazy and I run away as often as possible." (Recently, he and Mark jointly bought an old house for weekend getaways in the country in upstate New York, cheap but in need of big-time repair.)

As for an unpartnered life, Wayne says, "I'm not always sure whether I'm primarily horny so I have a person over for sex, or primarily lonely and just realize that getting a trick is the easiest way to have someone to spend time with." The Internet allows a person to create any number of different profiles, a phenomenon that Wayne takes advantage of. "If I want someone just to share my bed, I can advertise for exactly that—that I'm looking for someone to spend the night—and they do and they leave the next day, and I feel satisfied and it's no more complicated than that."

One of the attractions of Greenwich Village was and still is its neighborhood character. "There's very little excuse for not going out," Wayne says. "I go downstairs and there are a lot of things I can do in my neighborhood by myself. After living here for ten years, I inevitably run into someone I know if I walk along Christopher Street. The amount of energy I have to expend in order to be social is close to zero.

"But I do have a tendency to hibernate unless someone calls and says, 'Let's go for a walk or a bite to eat.' When Mark is in town, he's that person, which is ironic since I'm more the extrovert than he is. I'm perfectly happy to stay home, and really don't feel that I need to get out, say, just because it's the weekend. Sometimes I don't leave the house at all for two solid days, which I know isn't healthy—not *every* weekend, at least.

"I'm not resistant to going out the door, but I often don't unless someone takes me. I just order delivery in and stay home, especially when you can have the sex delivered, too."

And, though the story of the Central American trip remains unfinished, the novel that Wayne started on that trip, which he has titled *Hard*, is being published in spring 2006.

◆　　　◆　　　◆

Mark Sullivan, Wayne's friend and frequent traveling companion, writes: "Ironically enough, Wayne is most at home when he is traveling. Something inside him wakes up when he is placed in the middle of an unfamiliar environment. Even mundane things, like riding a bus, fill him with joy.

"Wayne is an extremely independent person, as are his brother and sister. I think this comes from their parents, who insisted that they all pick their own path. As a result, the people Wayne is closest to are all similar in that they haven't traveled in a straight line."

Volunteering and Exercising to Stay Young: Janet Bensu

Janet Bensu, in her early seventies, is no late sleeper or stay-at-home. Her day starts before dawn, exercising at a health club or setting out on various volunteer commitments in and around her San Francisco home. But the scope of her volunteering took a large geographical leap in January 2005 when Janet traveled with other volunteers to India in a group organized by the California Institute of Integral Studies. In a tour that initially focused on spirituality, the Americans headed to the Chanai area (Madras) and stayed in a micro village in Auroville, an international community built by people from around the world with land given to them by the Indian government. The theme of that community is peace and togetherness.

Quite unexpectedly, the visit took a turn away from the emphasis on spirituality or tourism. Arriving only weeks after the devastating tsunami in December 2004, Janet's group departed the community and traveled to a nearby village that had suffered huge destruction and the loss of dozens of lives. That's when eleven ordinary, not so young, American travelers became aid workers. "We hadn't set out to do that," Janet says. "That was never in our plan, but we all felt we'd like to do something if the occasion presented itself...and it did." That first visit turned into several, as the group returned to the damaged village again, helping to remove debris from the roads covered with bricks and concrete and wood from homes that had been destroyed.

"It was very hot," Janet says, "and we were looking at a huge task. We put only a dent in it, but doing that was a way to meaningfully help others. One of the women and I also visited a school where many of the children were tsunami victims, and we played games with them. Doing those things made the trip."

There were—and continue to be—material contributions to the Indian villagers whom Janet's group met. "While the tour was there," she says, "we went through our belongings and put together an impressive array of clothing. There are 250 families who live in that small area and who have lost so much, and we e-mailed family and friends at home asking them to pledge money to help in the relief." Back home, Janet reports, some members of the tour remain in touch with the Indian families and continue to send money as they are able to collect it.

◆   ◆   ◆

Even in San Francisco, Janet is home very little and inactive even less. Part of that is due to Eloise, a 32-lb. Tibetan terrier and Portuguese water dog mix. To say that Eloise helps get Janet out is way short of doing justice to the animal, who not only partners her on regular visits to elderly folks and hospitalized children but barrels into the hospital room and (with permission) occasionally crawls in bed with the kids. "The dog loves it," says Janet, "and I don't have to worry about whether I'm welcome. With her, I always am."

Janet's goodwill hospital calls are the latest in a long line of volunteer work. "I started off working with immigrants from Russia during a big surge of immigration in the 1980s," she says. "I did it consciously, to develop an extended family. Then, toward the end of that decade, I did practical support—shopping and cooking and cleaning—for AIDS patients confined to home. I'm still friendly with those who survived, but that work was hard, of course, because many of them died. Now I help two people with disabilities."

Along the way came Eloise. "She was a foundling, a rescue dog. I'm not even sure how old she is—we figure around eight. I took her to the park and began to meet other dog walkers. A woman there told me that she took her dog to visit sick people, and, she said, 'Eloise would be perfect for this.' I called the SPCA, and that led into what Eloise and I have been doing together for three years."

Janet has visited both old and young, and while she likes older people who "have kept some of their social skills," the best, she says, the very best, are the kids. "Some are just there for a broken leg or the like, so I know they're going to be all right. Others who look sicker are hard for me, but I right away establish whether they're gonna live. I ask, 'Is this one gonna get out of here?' When I know they're going to survive, I'm relieved."

Janet's affection for kids comes in part because they rarely complain. "They kind of know they're sick because they're in a hospital, but often they don't know the extent of it, so unless they are very sick they're usually perky with great spirit. They meet Eloise, who has one of those personalities that kids love. Maybe the kids have dogs, too, so they tell you about theirs and there are smiles all around."

"There are many benefits to those visits," Janet says. "They make me appreciative of my own life, my good health. And I feel that I've brought a little joy to someone else and am proud and pleased that I did it. I see how lonely life is for so many people who don't have the choices I have—to be healthy, active, and out with others."

It's clear that those visits give a needed spark to Janet's life. "Still," she adds, "those hospital visits fill me, and when I leave someone I've been with, whether the person was old or young, I think, 'Wow, I can be by myself now.'"

"I'm not a person who wants to be isolated," Janet says. "I enjoy dealing with people in my volunteer work, but I've also discovered that I really do like being my own boss, not having to make the compromises you must make when you live with someone. That adds up to being alone."

After time outside as a hospital volunteer, Janet retreats home to Reilly, her cat, assigned as inside watch guard while she and Eloise venture out. The dog collapses for a nap and Janet turns to knitting sweaters or scarves as gifts for friends, or maybe venturing out once more for classes at the Fromm Institute for Retired People. She lives a programmed day.

◆   ◆   ◆

If it's hard to locate a native New Yorker, it's scarcely easier to find a native Californian. Janet found her way from East Coast to West, although the trajectory for her was roundabout, starting in New York, her original home, thence to England, and following that, a detour to Turkey. "I was sent by IBM to England to do computer-related work," she says, "and I met my future husband there. He is Turkish, so we went back and forth between London and Istanbul. But he didn't want to stay in Turkey and neither of us was a citizen of Great Britain, so it was sort of like, where should we live? We came to this country, bought a car, drove all the way west to Northern California, and when we came over the Golden Gate Bridge, he said, 'This is where I want to be.' I said, 'Great, it's where I want to be, too.'"

Despite the city's can't-make-up-its-mind-how-the-weather-will-be-not-only-the-next-day-but-in-the-next-half-hour character, San Francisco long ago lost tally of the new arrivals on whom it has cast its spell. That included Janet and her husband who settled into a home by the bay until their marriage ended in divorce in 2003 (more or less amicably, she says). "To be settled successfully in San Francisco, I realized that I had to stop comparing it to New York," Janet says. "Each city is great, but they're very different. Once I accepted that, I was really happy to be here."

Given that her marriage lasted thirty years, it's not hard to question Janet's conviction that she is a solitary person who needs ample time alone. But she's determined about the idea. "Too much interaction over a long while exhausts me," she insists. "If I'm with a lot of people over extended time and have had little time for myself, I need to refuel—read or take a long walk. Just from that perspective, being married was difficult. If you have those kinds of days—and for me there were a lot—you realize that being alone is really not a bad thing."

Life in San Francisco helps her sustain that picture. "I don't know if it's a reality, but it seems to be easier to be alone here, or to escape it when I want to. If I get lonely, I go to the gym and there are lots of people to interact with. Here they're more accessible than in New York where everyone seems to be absorbed in their own lives. Or if I feel the need to talk to others, I take the dog to the beach, which isn't far away, and where there's a whole community of dog walkers. Then I'm glad to go home again. It's a lifestyle that's easy to manage in San Francisco, and I'd find it hard to give up now."

Across either of the bridges in and out of San Francisco are suburbs with an allure that draws scores of people, but Janet is not one. "I'm a city person, and I don't yearn to escape it," she says. "If you're in the suburbs and you want to go to the symphony or ballet, it means crossing a bridge and battling traffic." Maybe conditioned by her big city origins in New York, Janet says she walks a lot and uses her car only an estimated 20 percent of the time she goes out. "Of course," she chuckles, "San Francisco is a little different from New York for walking. We have hills."

◆   ◆   ◆

Newly single and with her house sold, Janet moved to a three-bedroom apartment, part of which she rents to another woman. "She's only a tenant. We don't share a lot or even see each other much, but having no children and no close relative nearby, I'm glad to have someone who would know if I didn't get up in the morning."

But she always does, and early. By her own reckoning, Janet's energy is compressed into the first hours of the day, and by evening she doesn't want to discuss anything, one more factor that worked against a successful marriage. The schedule she sets out on might shame many younger women and men. Blessed, in fact, with drive atypical for someone in their early seventies, many of her friends *are* younger women and men with whom she goes for hikes or bike rides.

For years Janet has been compulsive about physical exercise, with a trim figure to confirm the fact. "I had an automobile accident a few years ago," she reports, "and the doctor said, 'The reason you came out of it so well is that you were in good physical condition.' So the necessity of exercise is implanted in my head." She works out at a gymnasium connected to the University of San Francisco, and she takes pride in doing no less than what the university students are doing. Her visits are divided between aerobics three days a week and swimming the other three, all wrapped up by the hour when some others are opening their window shades. "Since my routine starts so early, I'm home before 9 AM and then I have the rest of the day left."

The gym at the university has a large pool, and people are attracted to it because of the pool facilities. For Janet, moving through the water is a recent undertaking, but it has become habitual and she has joined many others who find in swimming benefits mental as well as physical. "When I shower after swimming I feel so elated—I could do anything," she says. Approaching the sport in her own determined way, she worked her way up to be a member of the gym's Masters Swim Team after only six months in the pool. "They asked me if I'd be interested in joining the Masters Class, where you enter competitions against people in your age group. They needed swimmers in mine. 'OK,' I thought. 'It should be an adventure.'"

Thus, in April 2004, she joined her team on a trip to nearby Santa Cruz for a three-day meet with swimmers all from Northern California. The first race in which she competed was the first race of the meet, a mile distance. The next day was a three-quarters-mile race and the following day a half-mile race. As the tournament was ending on the last day and she was dressed and ready to leave, Janet was told that she had been added to the last event, a four-person relay. "I wasn't sure how well that would work, since the three others in the relay were in the fifty-five-to-sixty age group, at least ten years younger than myself. But they wanted me to do it, so I quickly changed back into my suit and got partnered up with the younger women. They were very kind to me, we gave it our all, and we came in first." Janet was so elated that with a couple of days' rest, she was looking ahead to the next three-day race in June.

Swimming has brought Janet new and welcome acquaintances. "Swimming is something people can do at any age. A woman of seventy-six has taught me how to face competition calmly and even to improve my strokes. She's someone to look up to, very upbeat and positive. She has several physical problems, but they don't stand in the way of her performing in a meet. The younger women say that I'm a role model for them. They like my energy and, in fact, during my first competition when I roomed with two women in their thirties, they actually went to bed before me."

◆   ◆   ◆

Aside from visiting people in nursing homes or hospitals, there are two disabled individuals whom Janet serves as personal shopper. One is a sixty-year-old woman who suffers from multiple sclerosis, is restricted to a wheelchair and rarely gets out. "She was a copywriter who lived in New York, a delightful, interesting person," says Janet. "Every week she e-mails me her shopping list and because she's on SSDI and doesn't have a lot of money, I sometimes go to four or five different stores to find her the best buys. I don't mind. There have been times when I've bought small pieces of furniture for her." Being computer savvy and stuck at home, the woman spends a lot of time on the Internet. "You can get crazy with buying things there, so I try to control her shopping and help her decide when she really needs something."

The other person whom Janet aids as shopper is a woman somewhat brain damaged. Since she is mobile, however, Janet drives her around to shop at different places. "She really has no money, and I don't know how she survives," Janet says. "The reason she's brain damaged is that she's bi-polar and the doctor prescribed the wrong dosage of lithium. She's such a sad case."

◆   ◆   ◆

Though she runs on a vigorous schedule and seems in exceptional health for someone in her eighth decade, Janet says that being alone does occupy her mind more as she ages. Her principal lifeline, as for many older and younger single persons, is the set of friends who live nearby and become dependable players in her life. Rhonda, a woman in her late thirties, Janet calls "the closest person to a daughter that I could have." Rhonda was twenty-one when Janet met her and her roommate. They would come to Janet's house for Sunday dinners and Janet kept up the friendship when the roommate left. "Over the years we've gotten closer," Janet says. "Rhonda refers to me as her surrogate mother and we celebrate Mother's Day together. That kind of relationship didn't happen accidentally; I've worked at establishing it."

Rhonda is married now, and Janet says that she is close to Rhonda's husband, Lukas, as well. "But Rhonda and I, the two of us, meet frequently for dinner to chat and catch up. I cherish her. We are even considering investing in property together."

It's plain that one of Janet's big pluses is her skill at meeting and keeping friends. Phyllis, her roommate from college in Ohio, lives across country in Manhattan, but she and Janet have stayed in touch for decades, traveling together and speaking by phone. Several of the past years, Janet has celebrated the Jewish High Holidays by going to New York so, she says, "that my friend and I could hang out together through the services."

According to Phyllis, Janet's trips east, aside from celebrating Yom Kippur with her and her family, are mostly to keep her away from food on that day of fasting. "I hate to fast," Phyllis says, "have always hated it, but Janet and I set our own rules for Yom Kippur. Janet insists on a simple sip of coffee to start the day, saying that, after that, she'll be fine. I tell her that fasting does not include a morning sip of coffee. But the rest of the day she has to put up with my talking about food and asking what time it is." Together they make the long day go by, try to think pious thoughts while catching up on each other's lives and waiting for the first stars to come into the sky, the traditional end of the holiday. "Then," says Phyllis joyfully, "we go to a 'break the fast' dinner together."

Phyllis, who sometimes returns the favor by traveling west to visit Janet, raises subjects that her friend seems to skirt. One concerns the fact that Janet had a successful career with giant companies in the computer field and later struck out and developed her own software business. When it grew to becoming an attractive purchase, Janet sold it for stock in the successor company. That proved to be a bad decision because eventually the new company collapsed, the owner went to prison, and the stock she had received lost most of its value. But, says Phyllis, it scarcely affected her spirit.

The two women have been close for so many decades that both are sure the other is a friend for life. "But she's in New York," Janet points out. "As for Rhonda and Lukas, I know they would help if I needed it. But I realize that while they're here now, there's no guarantee that they're going to stay in San Francisco. If you live alone and don't have children, these *are* concerns.

"Living alone isn't an all black or white issue. I'm not thinking of marriage, but I would like an occasional male companion, since often I don't want to go somewhere by myself. Sometimes I accept invitations and then come up with an excuse not to go—which is really a bad thing to do. Other times, I may force myself into the situation where I'll see other people. When I make myself go out, I often have a very good time, that is, if I put myself out and socialize even without knowing anyone there to start."

Janet looks ahead, staying with the volunteer work, reserving enough time for herself, and trying to look upon birthdays as a factor but not an impediment. Her view of the future also includes not only continuing visits to the gymnasium but competitive swimming, an undertaking made at an age when most people jump into a pool mostly to feel the warmth of water around them and advance no farther than the shallow end. In fact, Janet's speed in the spring 2004 swim meet gave her a benchmark to work from in the days ahead. "I saw people in their early *nineties* at that swim meet!" she states with eyes sparkling and—one might surmise—an itch to do the same.

That possibility, one realizes, is Janet's likely future. In the meantime, she lives a full day with volunteering and exercising and even the occasional unexpectedly enlightening trip like the one she took to India.

◆   ◆   ◆

Phyllis Goldman, Janet's long-time friend, says: "Janet has had to overcome some major setbacks, the collapse of both her marriage and that new company, plus estrangement from her only brother and his wife. Maybe she compensates for those things by having each part of her day well scheduled. She's about as organized and capable as anyone I've ever known."

Dancing, to Adopting:
Jodi Moccia

Nanjing is an inland town south of Beijing in the middle of China. It doesn't appear on the typical tourist map for Americans, but after two visits it's almost as familiar to Jodi Moccia, a dance choreographer, as her home town of Manhattan. As a result of her first ten day trip there in 1998, Jodi flew back across the Pacific carrying the object of the visit: a thirteen-month-old baby daughter whom she named Annais. Jodi made her second trip five years later, in 2003, with Annais along. After a stay of two more weeks, mother and daughter returned home with a thirteen-month-old baby sister for Annais, named Sage by her new mother. Annais is seven-and-a-half in 2005, a third grader with a bent for science. Sage (who renamed herself Ying Ying) is at two-and-a-half a kid who seems fearless, strong, and Jodi says may be ripe for gymnastics.

No husband participated in the research, planning, or actual adoption of either Annais or Ying. A former dancer, tall, lean, and beautiful, and unmarried for her fifty years, Jodi took care of all of that herself, costs included. Is she then a devotee of the single life? Though her reply is short of blissful, when comparing herself to mothers who are not alone, she says that it's good not to have someone telling her how she should raise her daughters. It's nice having total say on that matter herself, she believes. She does benefit from three single male friends on board as adopted uncles, as effective in spoiling young girls as a dad would be.

Annais, the older girl, was named Xiao at the orphanage. Jodi chose her Western name after Anais Nin, the French writer. "I've kept Xiao for her middle name," Jodi says. "I loved seeing 'A.X.M.' on a suitcase." Ying was the name given to the younger girl by the orphanage; her American name, Sage, was suggested by a fellow worker of Jodi's. That makes her full name Sage Ying Moccia. "I've done both," Jodi explains, "given them Western names and kept their original Chinese names for their middle names."

With her experience as an adoptive mother, Jodi puts forth firm advice for a single woman contemplating adoption overseas, especially in China. "Do it," she states, emphatically. "If you're only thinking about it, you're wasting time. Adoption of a Chinese baby never was simple, but lately their government has made it even harder for single women. There's a list you have to get on now if you're single. That means there's a waiting list before you can even be put on the list. Once you're there and your paperwork is done, you still have to wait a year, so the whole process could go on for three years."

The story of Jodi's adoptions may be more than usually complicated. "I thought a lot about whether or not to have a baby, especially as I was getting older," she recalls. "I had many conversations about it with a good friend, but the conversation never really got finished because in 1996, I started bleeding very heavily. I went to my doctor, she examined me and then granted me a week to do what I needed to do before going into the hospital. It was a shock. I almost had no time to think, which may have been a good thing."

As a little girl Jodi says she always felt that she was going to die young. When it was discovered that she had cancer requiring surgery, she was sure that moment had come. "I took care of everything that had to be done, but about five minutes before going into the operating room, I was ready to flee. I thought to myself, 'Just get up, walk out the door, and die. It'll be easier.' A nurse came over at that point, and I told her, 'I'm leaving. I'm going out the door now, so take these tubes out of me.' The nurse said, 'No, you're not. You're going to lie down here and you're going to go into *that* door, and you're going to come out and you're going to be OK.' The next thing I knew I was in the operating room and immediately was out. When I woke up, it was over. I had made it. I didn't have to die at forty-one."

The hysterectomy that Jodi underwent at an early age left her peaceful and happy. Though it settled the question of whether or not to have children, that issue was still on her mind, and she decided to sign up as a "big sister." The first meeting didn't work for her. "They kept stressing that big sisters don't commit: that is, the child put in your care has a mother and a home, so while you spend the day with her and show her your world, at the end of the day the child goes to her home, not yours. I never went past that first meeting because I knew it wouldn't be for me. Commitment was exactly what I did want."

Jodi went on the Internet and researched adoption possibilities—in Russia, in South America, and then in China. "When I read about the opportunities in China, my whole body just went, 'Oooh.' After that, it was easy. I got in touch with someone who had gone there, and she gave me the name of an agency in Massachusetts run by two women who really want to get babies out of that country. The one I contacted was wonderful. She led me through the steps needed to send off my first application letter, never asking whether I was going to use her or talking about money at all. I kept shooting forth questions and finally, three months later, I told her that I would use her agency. Her answer was simple: 'OK.' I knew it was the right place to be. That proved to be even more true when I set out for the second adoption. Every other agency, including those of our own government, had raised their fees, but not the women in Massachusetts."

It was a year after mailing her first letter that Jodi boarded a plane to Asia. The agency had arranged everything beforehand, she says, including an introduction in Chinatown in Manhattan to a woman who would receive her when she arrived in China. Jodi asked Ellen Ratner, a good friend, to go with her. "We went first to Nanjing where the agency has a fine hotel and where doctors are nearby. The next day we boarded a bus and drove three hours through rice fields to the tinier town of Heifei, to the adoption agency. Even after all that, I guess part of me still wasn't ready for meeting my baby. I passed a woman in the hall who was holding a child. I kept on going, but the woman stopped me and said, 'Jodi, this is your daughter.'"

"What!" Jodi recalls thinking. "The baby was sleeping. I took her in my arms, she sort of nuzzled in my shoulder, and when she finally woke up, we had our first look at each other. When I looked at her, she glanced away, and when I looked away, she would stare at me. I was obviously different from the people she had known."

There was more to do before they could come home. Says Jodi, "Once you get the baby, there's Chinese paperwork—passport and adoption papers. We did that in Nanjing. Then, when that's done, you go to Guangzhoz to the American Embassy to get the baby's visa. That all takes time. I finally got back to New York with Annais on Christmas Eve 1998. And just a couple of days later, I was on a train with the baby to Virginia to pick up my job, because during all of that I was working as an associate choreographer."

Seven years have passed since Jodi became a parent and undertook raising one, and then a second, little girl in Manhattan, a challenge for any woman, single or married. After starting her in a private school ("expensive and not very fine"), Jodi transferred Annais to a nearby public elementary school that is part of New York City's Education Department. "That school is wonderful," Jodi glows. "Without making her self-conscious about it, they focus very quickly on where the child needs help, in Annais's case, with reading. Now I hear her say, 'I don't wanna watch TV, I'm gonna go read.' It's amazing!

"The teachers are great, but a lot of why the school is good is how much parents are involved. If there's a support-team feeling between parents, the kids pick up on it, and I think that's why Annais has improved so much this year. Parents take turns coming to read to the kids. I chose a dance story so I could demonstrate steps described in the book. I showed the boys how some of the sports they like use the same movements as in dance. They loved it."

Jodi enjoys support from other mothers aside from the adopted uncles. One is a woman she met in nearby Connecticut who was going to China to adopt a baby at the time Jodi went for her first trip. "She told me that we had to pack six baby bottles. 'Why six?' I asked. 'Do we really need to bring *six* baby bottles?' 'Yes,' she said, 'you have to pack six. One is for the baby, and the other five are filled with vodka for us.' Needless to say, we've remained friends, and now our four little Chinese girls are friends, too."

Jodi believes that the two sides of her life, working and child rearing, balance each other well. She describes herself as a woman who gets crazy when she isn't at work, though working serves for more than just achieving a happy balance: it becomes vital for raising her children. Jobs for a freelance choreographer are sporadic and often brief, and having money for child care poses the real challenge. "I like my work, but I also get out and push for those jobs because I need the income," Jodi says. "It isn't shoe money, or food money, it's money for child care that really costs. That's the hard part of this picture."

◆   ◆   ◆

Along with a book to read to Annais's class, Jodi brings dance shoes for the children to see and feel: toe shoes, tap shoes, ballet slippers. They have been among her belongings since she started ballet lessons at age eleven. "My mother had a good friend, Marjorie Marshall, who had a dance school here in Manhattan," Jodi says. "The school only taught tap and acrobatics, but Marjorie wanted to expand it and teach ballet. She thought that with my body type I could go to a ballet school, learn some, and then come back and teach it at her school.

"When my mother told me this, I cried, 'I'm not going to some stupid ballet school,' but that didn't matter because I was quickly sent off to the Christine Newbert School of Ballet. The girls were looking at me because I was in black tights and they were all in pink. I was dying. But then I went into the classroom and met the teacher, Barbara Walzack. She was so beautiful, and then she started to dance. When I walked out of the class, the first thing I said to my mother was, 'I want to become a ballet dancer.' Miss Newbert said that with a lot of hard work I could do it, so I started lessons seriously right then. Later, I actually did go back to teach at Marjorie Marshall's school.

"Miss Walzack told me about the High School of Performing Arts. I knew my dad wouldn't willingly let me go there, so I purposely failed the test to go to a Catholic school. The only high school I made was Performing Arts, so he had no choice but to let me go. Unfortunately, he died before I got to tell him my scam."

In 1974, at age nineteen, Jodi joined the Alvin Ailey Dance Company, which employs many, but not exclusively, African-American dancers. She remained with Ailey for four years, but by then, she says, she felt beat up. "It was tough, tough being on the road, having that kind of life. And there was so much pressure. Like everyone else, I was injured a lot, but if you walked in on crutches because you'd banged up your toe, no one cared. They only wanted to know when you'd be ready to perform again."

Jodi quit the dance company and tried runway modeling because fashion shows were using dance steps. But at every audition, she says she rebelled at being just a figure, knowing that she had a head that was going unused. "That experience made me realize that I still wanted to dance and to try to say something there. The modeling lasted only six months."

It was a crossroads for Jodi, a choice of heading to the drugstore to get a job or going to dance auditions. She put away her pride and decided to try auditioning; it brought her a spot in Bob Fosse's *Dancin' on Broadway* in 1979. "*Dancin' on Broadway* was a three-act musical of numbers that Bob wanted to do," Jodi says. "It was an evening of just dance, no book, a variety of different kinds of music, like the show, *Fosse*, that was on Broadway a few years ago. I was an alternate, which meant that I understudied all the women in the show, even did some boys' parts if there were too many injuries. It was the best, because I never got bored from doing the same thing every night.

"*Dancin* was my first work on Broadway, and it led to commercials and movies and TV shows. Those are lucrative but they're short-term. If you're lucky and are in a show on Broadway that's a hit, you have an income for awhile. But hits are rare. I met a man who lived in Los Angeles and I decided to move there because of him and see how I liked working there. It took me about a year to realize that the relationship wasn't going to last and that I wanted to be back in New York. So I moved back."

In 1983 Jodi met famed choreographer Michael Bennett and was hired to work with him and Bob Avian on *Scandal*, a show with a workshop production that lasted a year. "In *Scandal* I was a dancer again, with Jerry Mitchell as my dance partner. The story was about a couple going through their seven-year itch, with the man having affairs left and right, the woman who had only been with one man, her husband, deciding to go off to discover other possibilities all around the world. That was the most fun I had in my life—dancing, living, learning, and playing. Jerry and I danced so well together, we ended up showing everyone else how to do it. We were making up steps while we went along. One time Michael said to me, 'You have something, and you should think about choreographing.' He made us associate choreographers—he was the one who started me moving to the other side of the footlights."

Jodi has remained close friends with Jerry Mitchell, an award-winning choreographer today. After *Scandal* she became associate choreographer on *Sunset Boulevard*, *Never Gonna Dance*, *Gypsy*, and, especially, *Miss Saigon*. "I've been associate choreographer of the Broadway, national, and international companies of *Miss Saigon*," she says. "There's a new company where I'm credited as choreographer that's been out on the road for three years, starting its fourth in fall 2005. *Miss Saigon* has been a cash cow for me; that's how I got my adoption money and enough to buy an apartment." Jodi also pitches in as a volunteer in organizing *Broadway Bares*, a fund-raising theatrical event featuring Broadway dancers that Jerry Mitchell directs.

As a single mother, Jodi gets to exercise her instinct to run things, and it's an instinct that carries over into her professional life. Being choreographer on the road company of *Miss Saigon* fits exactly with her goal of the last two years. "I finally had enough of being the associate," she says. "I'd gotten to the point where I thought, no, I don't want to do the step that you want to do, I want to do it *this* way. It was time to become the choreographer and not the associate or assistant."

She has a clear vision of what is required for her to be successful as a show's choreographer. "What form of dance to use isn't what I need, because I end up mixing ballet with jazz and tap. It's all dance. What I need is for the story and the characters' stories to be where I can envision what to add so they continue reaching their peak. If talking and singing haven't completed the character, we have to move into the physical state. At that point, it's easier for me to create the dance steps. Numbers flow right out of me, and I never really change them. Other numbers I can work on for days.

"It's a big step to leave behind not only dancing but the associate choreographer title. The job of choreographer is very competitive, and that's where the stress comes in. In the beginning, it's like starting all over again because you're in what's for you a new field. You have to do freebees to get known, just as you did when you were a young dancer. I've gotten an agent in Los Angeles and that should help me on Broadway, as she's bi-coastal. But I've also gotten together my DVD to submit for commercials and movies. It's snippets from work I've done."

Exuding the confidence and energy that fueled her urge to adopt children and buy an apartment as a single woman—and continue carving new careers—Jodi adds, "Right now I feel as if I've planted a lot of seeds in different places; it's gotten busy and I'm not sure which job to do next!"

♦   ♦   ♦

Patricia Masters, Jodi says, is her close friend whom she met as a young girl when they were on scholarship at the Alvin Ailey school and taking dance classes together. The two women lost touch until a decade ago when they reconnected by a chance meeting in a dance class. Patricia was a psychic and Jodi asked her for a reading. For the next two years, Patricia met with her and gave her readings in which she stressed that her friend needed to be prepared to not do things in the conventional way that many others do. "Patricia," Jodi says, "was the one who saw blockage and told me to see a doctor. I did go, and the first time I was fine, but she urged me to keep going back. Though it was a shock, of course, when I got the news about needing surgery, there was a bit of a cushion already there."

Later, when she decided to adopt, Jodi went back to tell Patricia. "'You've got it!' Patricia said. 'That's what I've been talking to you about.'"

Jodi has been around show business long enough to know that it's never a nine-to-five world. "When you have a job, you're looking for your next one," she says. "There are times full and times lean, and you need to save your money when there is work for the times when there isn't." Discussing with Patricia her moments of anxiety about work, Patricia said that they needed to find a way for Jodi to relax and make those the times to refuel. "She asked me, 'When were you the happiest?' I said that it was right after that bout with cancer. She said for me to tap into it. I closed my eyes and tried to recapture those moments, and I immediately felt calm. I started to hang on to that 'happy place.' That's where I go when I need to, to my happy place. Leading me that way, Patricia gave me an invaluable gift."

♦   ♦   ♦

In both face and figure, Jodi looks much less than her half-century age, healthy, energetic, and easily in reach of that "happy place." "I do everything possible to keep in shape," she says. "Sometimes it's dance class, sometimes swimming, sometimes running. If I do one thing all the time, I find I don't do it any more. In the summer I swim, in the fall I love running in Central Park, in the winter I take dance classes all wrapped up in wool sweaters and socks."

Together with Annais and Ying, Jodi lives today in a duplex garden apartment near Carnegie Hall, a neighborhood filled with musicians and artists, in every way the other side of the globe from a Chinese orphanage. "What makes me love my place is the chance to walk outside into a garden that's large enough for a table and chair and a kiddie's swimming pool," says Jodi. "Upstairs is a living room with an open fireplace and a kitchen. I use that a lot, as I love to cook. Downstairs is basically an open space but large enough that we can build walls and create different rooms when the girls get bigger and we all need privacy. I was really lucky in buying the apartment. It was in February 2000 when I had just the first kid and before prices in the city went berserk."

Raising adopted Chinese girls in New York City is a way of life today, according to Jodi. "I am constantly meeting people in the street with Chinese kids. They stop and ask what province my girls are from. We swap stories, and the kids meet each other. There are two families like that just on my street, and a lot in Annais's school. These girls seem happy and well-adjusted and well loved, maybe because their mothers went to some trouble to get them!"

Besides being a mother, Jodi is a protective daughter. Her own mother, now eighty and "strong as a bull," comes by from her apartment in Riverdale, in the Bronx, as an occasional baby sitter but only when the summer heat is not severe. "I give a lot of credit to my mother for supporting my wish to study dance and for working to provide me with those ballet classes a long time ago. She had been a secretary before she was married, and she gave up that career to marry. When my sister and I got older, Mom wanted to go back to work, and she did. She has never pushed me or my older sister toward marriage. My father was a butcher and then a bar and restaurant owner, not around a lot. He wasn't crazy about my being a dancer, though that got better when I joined Ailey and he saw that I was part of a reputable troupe. He passed away from a heart attack when he was about fifty.

"My parents raised me as a Catholic, but the truth is that when I was little and went to church, I had a hard time thinking of sins to confess. I had to work to come up with something, but it wasn't very dramatic." As for religion for her daughters, Jodi doesn't have an answer now. "They come from a different culture, of course, but this is the only culture they know. The only place they've had a life is here, and Annais states that she is an American. Until they're older and can check it out for themselves, the religion I teach them is to do unto others, don't lie, keep learning to share, and take care of each other. And love all."

Even with all the spunk and optimism that Jodi exudes, a visitor questions whether her life must not seem top heavy with duties of mother and father. After a moment's thought, she refigures the question and then gives the answer. "Are there times when the girls are being brutal to each other and fighting and screaming and I go, 'Why did I do this?' Of course. I've said it a million times. But I certainly don't feel as if I've made a mistake, getting these two kids. I don't feel that way at all.

"One day, when they're older, I would like to take them back to show them the country where they were born. But they'll grow up to be American like me, and right now I look at them and think, 'Remember that place you came from? The future there looked pretty bleak. Here you are now, living in a garden apartment in America, standing in midtown Manhattan, hailing a cab.'

"They're as much mine as if they had always been, so it's been a two-sided deal. If I've saved their lives, they've saved mine, too."

◆   ◆   ◆

Jerry Mitchell, Jodi's former dance partner and still good friend, writes: "Jodi's passion for what she does, and her discipline as part of her dance training, are two of the greatest qualities she is passing on to her girls. So many people get confused with what really counts when bringing up children. When you raise them with love, discipline and passion for life…those are such wonderful qualities coming from any parent."

Just Staying Solo: Stanley Ely

I was a teenager in Texas through the staunchly conventional late1940s, and I belonged to a staunchly conventional Jewish crowd. We wore white socks and penny loafers and attended Sweet Sixteen dances and everything else banded together as if we were some threatened tribe. Our parents worried that we were dissolute. I was so active a member of that bunch that you might have thought I was straight. I more or less thought so, too, despite fantasies of young men that propelled me into the bathroom while I locked the door and relieved some of the tension.

For me, those years, and even a while after, were a pool of denial. The contradiction between my socializing and fantasizing, between being in the world and being shuttered alone, both of which kept me busy, was something I didn't consider, much less acknowledge.

My coming out as gay man was a bumpy affair that started only in my mid-twenties, after college and a stint in Korea. If I had to submit to the draft, I figured Uncle Sam would send me to Europe. There was an unexpected advantage to the assignment in Korea, however: housing for wives and children didn't exist at that time, so our camp was exclusively male. I was exempt from the need to pretend hunting for female company. In fact, with no women nearby, I regret to think how many interesting opportunities I probably passed up.

The Army experience followed college, which followed my attachment to the teenage high-school crowd. By the time I graduated from Highland Park High in Dallas in 1949, a voice was telling me to get away and not just next door. I set my sights on Northwestern University in Evanston, north of Chicago, a part of the country I saw only when I arrived for class in the fall of 1950.

So I departed the Lone Star State early. The move north to college, and the time in the Army overseas that followed, led to my coming at twenty-four to New York and remaining here ever since. Though I've revisited Texas many times, those trips were to see family and friends, not to renew residence.

◆   ◆   ◆

I do believe, as demonstrated by others in this book, that people can go through contrasting stages in their lives—time with women, time with men, time living with others, and time living alone. I shared two apartments during my early years in Manhattan, but with that, plus long stretches in college dormitories and Army barracks, a wish for privacy took over, and I sought a permanent place by myself.

The seeds for my living alone actually were planted early. The story goes that when I was around age two, I developed a serious ear infection, which led to months of confinement in bed and no antibiotics available. Once recovered, I'm told, I had to re-learn to walk and began to cling to my mother's skirts. She concluded that I needed emancipation, so she absented herself for afternoons and left me with Marietha, my nanny, whom I loved and who didn't mind being clung to.

Later, when I was eight or nine, my parents started to leave me alone when they went out for the evening. "We let you stay by yourself much sooner than your older brother or sister," Mother said, so frequently that it sounded as if she were working to expel some guilt. But she needn't have bothered, since, by then, no one in the whole town would have been more agreeable to the idea than I. At nine, this boy couldn't have had a more fervent wish than to be ruler of the house for an evening.

It's not so different now. While I was teaching high school I was satisfied to end a day of facing teenagers with a quiet retreat to home, required to converse with no one besides my one and sometimes two cats. Now, past full-time teaching, I still find (with exceptions, to be sure) that I like turning away the rest of the world when I close my apartment door. If there are those whose terror is to be alone, I verge on the opposite. I'm the odd bird who doesn't even mind traveling by himself and often does so.

Like others in this book, today I enjoy the advantage of the unpartnered life—freedom to plan my day without the involvement of another person. It doesn't mean I'm a hermit. But the hours I spend solo, sometimes considerable, are hours necessary to get my head on straight before going out again in the company of others.

No doubt…if married life isn't automatically fulfilling, neither is the unpartnered life, as a great many unhappy single people would testify. You have to look for ways around it.

◆   ◆   ◆

My years at Northwestern in a group of fun-loving, mostly non-Jewish friends culminated in an undistinguished grade-point average but a degree in Spanish anyway. It wasn't long afterwards that I submitted to the Army's call, and two years later, I used the GI Bill to study Spanish in Mexico and Arizona.

By 1957, at age twenty-four, I was determined to come to New York to work in international advertising. I signed my first lease, for a $78 per month walk-up studio in Greenwich Village, and pestered a well-known ad agency until they offered me a job that paid almost as much as the rent. For the next dozen years I bounced with limited success around the world of advertising, marketing, and, in a nearly fatal move, export finance. I grew to hate the fact that I had gone to that last job, those few years turning into the darkest of my life. Finally, I realized that I had to go somewhere radically different if there was to be a chance for feeling content.

On a hunch, I risked leaving twelve years in the business world to embark on a teaching career. Being a teacher had never been in my plan, so I needed to go back to school for the education courses and eventually a master's degree. But I made my commitment, and at age thirty-six took a job commuting from Manhattan to a public high school in a nearby suburb. Nervously, I began to face a classroom in Spanish, and, later, with more study, in French. Teaching makes its own demands, but it enabled me to appreciate an element that had been missing during my years in business: the human dimension. It was over the next twenty years in the same school that I enjoyed the greatest satisfaction that I achieved in a workplace.

Since I started teaching relatively late, I was able to retire relatively young, and did so at age fifty-six. My plan was to write, a field in which I had dabbled in high school and college. Today writing is an important part of my life. Ask any writer, and he or she will agree that writing is one of the all-time solitary activities, so it seems as if writing and I found each other. It's gratifying to discover that even when the body ages (my first book got published when I was turning sixty-five), the creative mind doesn't have to follow. So I write, and am better at it today than years ago.

Writing and publishing are both slow processes, however, and I need other activities to bring me fulfillment. For me, as for many others, much of that has to do with volunteering.

I've had several volunteer jobs. The first was with an organization of gay and lesbian writers and editors. I shepherded a program called BookAIDS which provided overruns of novels to service agencies that handle HIV-positive clients. We began small, but BookAIDS grew to include half a dozen publishers shipping hundreds of books monthly to fourteen agencies around the country. The program, unfortunately, died out when publishing houses merged and backed away. While it lasted, many letters testified to the valuable service BookAIDS provided for persons living with the HIV virus.

During that same time, I volunteered at a health center in Manhattan. I checked people in and out and then began and, for a few years, continued to edit a newsletter, joining the center's board of directors along the way. My tenure on the board went on past a decade.

In early 2003 I joined an organization that provides tutors to New York City public schools and was assigned to a relatively new, small high school in East Harlem. I now go weekly to help eleventh- and twelfth-graders on essays to accompany their college applications. These young people, mostly Hispanic, are nervous about the process of college entrance since, in almost every case, they are the first in their family even to contemplate education beyond high school. Many of them came to this country poor, with no English-speaking skills, and often with a single parent. Discovering and putting their life stories on paper makes this one of the most gratifying experiences I've ever had.

Now, there are occasional dinner dates with friends besides many evenings at home with two cats, Sis and Honey, a TV set, book and computer. That's a scene that in times past I might have disparaged, but one that has become a not unpleasant part of my life—a sure byproduct of aging. I give into the temptation to while away time exploring the world of the Internet, plus using it to correspond in an easy but impermanent way with friends everywhere.

I know that too much at home becomes unhealthy. Recently I've been attending meetings of SAGE, a group for older gay men and women. It took awhile for me to own up to being the right age, but at SAGE I see how other men of my age, or younger, are dealing with aging and, in most cases, with living alone. Some of them flourish despite physical limitations; others, inert mentally and physically, scarcely cope at all. Those meetings are good laboratories for examples to be copied or to be skirted.

With a friend or two I subscribe to theatre companies (less expensive than going to Broadway shows) and I retain memberships in a few museums which I'm lucky to live near, so I try to keep up with new art exhibits. My address is also close to Central Park, and when I crave a dose of close-by nature, I head there on sunny days. I try to hold the weight in check by working out at a health club two or three times a week. And since I have lived for years in a rent-stabilized apartment, I save on the excruciating rent burden that newly arrived New Yorkers face. This has allowed me to indulge in those meals out and to make occasional trips to Europe, lately to visit Russia to see the country from which my mother and her family immigrated long ago.

◆   ◆   ◆

I believe that as some people accommodate themselves to marriage or live-in partners, others make sensible accommodation to living a fulfilling life alone. It doesn't just happen; it requires input and maybe exploration of why this lifestyle is what appeals or works best. I'm not alone in this book as a person who, in relationships that began to be serious, found himself with his own needs shirked. Fearful of the pain of losing my own identity (or perhaps not skilled in knowing how not to lose it), I've avoided intimacy. I'm not suggesting that bachelorhood is a second-class existence, but that it needs understanding and planning.

The intimacy that I don't have with a lover is replaced by a more limited kind with young people. I do private tutoring for high school students when I am able to, and working one-on-one with a teenage boy or girl seems to mobilize the generous, paternal side of me. Nearly always, the student improves academically, and we round out the months or sometimes years together with warm feelings. Maybe these relationships substitute for a nonexistent child or lover.

But there are risks, especially for an older, single gay man. The risk is developing too heavy an attachment, as happened not long ago with a boy I'll call Sam, with whom I met for several years for tutoring in French and who then quite suddenly called it quits. I've asked myself what caused his abrupt, unexpected departure. Was it the subject matter? Was it me?

There's another possibility. The previous spring Sam attended a play I had written—and he asked me later whether the gay character in the play was me. "Of course," I said, pleased that the young fellow felt comfortable raising the question. But maybe that interchange set off an alarm. Maybe the non-sexual closeness with an older gay man frightened a boy on the cusp of his sexual life. It's been an effort not to see Sam's need to quit as some fault of mine or that his leave taking carried a wish to wound.

Perhaps those of us who live alone—and continue to live alone—become more vulnerable to situations like this. Teachers especially are destined to experience a parting that can leave a serious gap if the student held a special place.

Not surprisingly, another Sam recently came along, so there will be another ending. But those attachments give me nourishment, and I don't close them out.

◆   ◆   ◆

Many times I wish I had grown up in a clan of artistic people to serve as models I could emulate—people whose daring unconventionality would ignite the same in me. But it didn't happen. Most everything in my house was middle of the road.

Lacking that beginning, I've been left to stir up my own dust, especially trying to establish a writing career well past the age when most writers begin theirs. And, after years of faking my sexual orientation, allowing it to come forward in my writing and my life.

By now, my nieces and nephews know of my homosexuality, colleagues know, and my students unless they're awfully slow have figured it out too, and I mean those other than Sam. The world knows who I am, and it hasn't fallen apart. With one exception, everyone I know is officially in the know. The exception is Uncle Morris, my mother's baby (and only) brother.

Recently turned ninety-six, my uncle lives in Dallas, still independently, and, like me, alone. Not what would have been called handsome even years ago, he is short, slender, brown-eyed and since early on mostly bald. Though age has caught up with him physically, senility hasn't come within miles of his address. My relationship with him moved into gear when he returned from service in World War II and for three or four years made our house his address (my mother's idea, of course). I was in high school and we shared a bedroom, above protests from me. What a pair we made: a nervous teenager rooming with a tense bachelor uncle. Later Morris moved out, and in his fifties he married and had an exceptionally happy marriage until Dorothy, his wife, died of cancer twenty-five years later.

Those years mellowed my uncle and, for me, time helped to do the same. Now, with Dorothy and my parents deceased, I telephone my uncle regularly and go back to Dallas once or twice a year to visit. Decades later, there we are together again, neither of us walking any too steadily. We're hardly a less unlikely pair than years ago, but the atmosphere lacks the old tension. He indulges his passion for sports and I, disinterestedly, listen to his commentary. We're congenial without prying.

Though Uncle Morris knows I'm a writer, I rarely speak of it, and if I do, he shows no interest. I've used him as subject matter for occasional columns in gay papers, but even if the columns are warmhearted, it is writing he hasn't seen.

Why, having opened my mouth to everyone, including to readers, do I section him off from a basic aspect of my life? When he makes his usual statement about any unmarried young man, "I don't understand why some girl hasn't grabbed him," I conclude that even the possibility of homosexuality is something my uncle doesn't grant a place at the table, that it's a subject banished from the agenda. So, though he must have figured it out long ago, I exclude any talk about that side of me.

In doing so, I say that I avoid forcing him into an uncomfortable confrontation. I've respected his limits and congratulate myself on my generosity. But my generosity is suspect. In respecting Uncle Morris, I have, in an odd way, insured that my limits are respected, also. We are none of us altogether consistent, so maybe I enjoy still keeping at least one person out of the loop. "Don't ask, don't tell," that unfortunate rule for the Armed Services, is, in a strange way, a practice that he and I have used to mutual benefit.

In Uncle Morris I have an example of someone whose fulfillment hasn't required volunteer work or teaching or most anything beyond earning money at cards, at which he was very successful, having a late, happy marriage, keeping his affairs in good order, and caring about the well-being of family. My uncle spends hours at home by himself, isolated by most people's standards but seemingly content. I suspect his moments of loneliness may be fewer than mine. In his final years, his needs are met by making meals, keeping a watchful eye on sports and the stock market, being dependent on as few people as possible and, in his words, "not telling other people how to live their lives." There must be worse formulas.

◆   ◆   ◆

Uncle Morris is the last living member of his family's generation. Of my dad's side, neither he nor any of his five siblings or his sibling's spouses survives.

I'm now without not only parents but siblings, since Jerome, my brother eight years older than I, died an untimely death from cancer years ago at age thirty-eight. My sister Florence, ten years older than I, died of cancer and stroke as she was nearing age seventy.

These events propelled me to publish a book called *In Jewish Texas: A Family Memoir* in 1998. I went to Texas to do readings, some before friends I had hardly seen since our high school days. There was no temptation to rejoin them, but trying to erase the intervening half century was for a little while a happy grabbing of nostalgia for me and them.

That book credited my parents with allowing me to go away to college, something that clearly began to shape the rest of my life. The book also dissected frustrations I had with family, probably not so different from most other humans. When I reconsidered my mother's wish to emancipate me at age three or four, it seemed more like desertion than emancipation, even if leaving me at home alone a few years later was, as I said, warmly welcomed. One goes through these peaks and valleys in a lifetime, and though I never achieved a loving relationship with my father, I did so with my mother. In the final years of her life, with time to reflect back, she said to me, "Stanley, I made so many mistakes years ago." I replied, "Well, they weren't important." Nothing was as important as my parents' strength to survive the critical event in our family, the death of my brother, Jerome, at a young age.

Jerome served in the Air Force in World War II, completed his education early, and moved to Stamford, Connecticut to work as an industrial psychologist. He married a young Jewish woman in 1954. I came to Manhattan on weekend leave from basic training in Georgia to serve as my brother's best man. In the next few years he and Paula, his wife, had two daughters, Elissa and Marcia.

In 1962, a point when my brother's life bubbled with success, a routine chest x-ray revealed a spot on one of his lungs. He entered treatment at a hospital in New Haven, and a friend of mine urged me to speak to one of his doctors. I did so, and heard a stunning, fatal prognosis.

It was hard to imagine that at age thirty-seven my brother could be struck by lung cancer, all the moreso since he had never smoked. The easiest reaction was to deny how serious his condition was, and denial quickly took hold as something of a motif in our family. I kept the doctor's prognosis to myself, and even I found myself walking a fine line between denial and the doctor's prediction. What was happening had a great sense of unreality, and perhaps allowing it to seem unreal helped us to get through it. In my mind was a mixture of disbelief and guilt as I watched the fading of a brother who was widely loved and who had been a constant mentor for me.

His death in February 1963, some nine months after that first chest x-ray, was as great a shock as had it taken place without warning. Although my brother's passing occurred over four decades ago, those days remain as vivid as if they happened yesterday, maybe more vivid than I would like. Only a few months after Jerome's death I fled the drug company where I was working to move to the export finance job, a change that at another time with clearer vision I would have known was a mistake. My tendency to live alone had been established earlier, and it is not something I regret, but it was certainly fanned by my brother's passing—maybe even responding to a need to stay alone as justification for staying alive.

◆   ◆   ◆

My father has now been gone for three decades, and I have nothing to irritate him about (principally the fact that I never married). Soon my mother will also have been gone for two decades. When I go to Dallas, I drive to an old part of town and visit the Shearith Israel Jewish cemetery that my paternal grandfather, Solomon Ely, helped found as a Romanian burial ground long ago. That's where my parents and my four grandparents are buried. The cemetery is a well-tended, shady place with birds often the only other intruders. I like to stroll around, passing the graves of parents of old friends, remembering fun and not especially dissolute parties in their homes, acknowledging the privileged way in which I grew up.

I bring flowers and arrange them on the gravestones of my parents and two sisters of my mother whom I loved dearly, Pearl and Fannie. There's a bench where I sit and talk to my parents, giving news of the family and myself. Part of my visit is to offer apologies to my father for the unrelenting anger I heaped upon him, an anger I had such difficulty letting go of. Finally, when an hour or so has passed and with a few tears shed, I wave good-bye and hope that my words somehow reach the spirits of those people who influenced me so deeply.

My mother regretted that as an adult I had pulled away from the Jewish traditions in which I was raised. I can hear her disappointment even now. Her regret stemmed not from a moral command but from the support she found that prayers gave to her and that she would have liked me to have, also. I am still not drawn back to those prayers or observances of the Jewish holidays, although I have a greater appreciation for Jewish history and, lately, a strong hunger for a spiritual connection to the universe and to my family's past.

A century ago, my father came as a little boy with his parents from Romania, and around the same time my mother at age eight and her parents and younger sisters fled a prosperous but pogrom-threatened life in Western Russia. They said good-bye to grandparents too old to travel, whom they knew they would never see again. Both families left their native lands to join uncles and cousins already settled in Houston, carrying only a few possessions and prayer and faith for a hoped-for better life. Later my parents married and remained in Texas. Neither went back or wanted to go back to see the countries they came from.

They made mistakes, but whatever those mistakes were, they set out and succeeded in building a family in America that was better educated and better cared for than they had been, and that they loved always.

◆   ◆   ◆

The speed with which the years pile one atop another becomes alarming. Though I'd be pressed to account for much of that time, I've now lived in Manhattan for well over forty years, in one apartment for over thirty. I am a great uncle a few times over.

How does the passing of time connect to relationships, the principal subject of this book? The state of living alone does not decree living without sex, something some might call a substitute for a relationship. A single person can look for sexual partners as much as desire and energy allow. I've taken advantage of this, seeking random sexual meetings more often than lasting connections. AIDS is now with us for two and a half decades, and if it hasn't gone away, a lot of my sexual potency has. Not altogether willingly, I've watched what was a salient feature of my life retreat to a secondary plane, leaving a vacuum replaced neither by partner nor really anything else. Fortunately, as one ages, there seems to be a correlation between the availability and the need for sex.

There are new challenges: to approach my final years without bitterness for a diminishing sex drive, the absence of a partner, the death of family members, and the early loss of close college friends. How to do that doesn't offer up an easy answer, and I'm not sure there is one. As someone who was the youngest of his family and for some time managed to look younger than his age, I have had to face the unwelcome but inescapable fact that appearance changes, the waist line enlarges, hands wrinkle in an ugly way, energy diminishes, and if you challenge Nature by trying to fake youth, you're taking on a formidable foe.

I readily acknowledge Uncle Morris's success in living alone, but I'm not ready to return to Texas or to be as isolated from the world as he is. So, while trying to balance time alone and time out in the world, I hold diminished expectations, attempt to keep to a reasonably healthy diet with exercise, continue volunteer work, allow myself to be devoted to the occasional teenager (but realize that they can change as fast as the wind), and keep close to friends and the younger generation of my family. On my map is an effort not to take myself too seriously (that one's hard). I also try to begin each day with a prayer of gratitude for a host of blessings, above all my health and my life in a free land. If I'm smart,

I keep in mind that I and everyone else I know are less than the tiniest point on history's map.

What about intimacy? Though I attempt to cultivate closeness with family and friends and some students, in these relationships I do withhold real intimacy, the step past closeness. In being with others, I leave unachieved the kind of intimacy gotten if you have built a successful partnership. Intimacy (maybe some would call it truthfulness) of that sort is barred with everyone but myself, where I try to leave it unblocked.

For someone who felt he'd been given a prize when he was left alone at age eight or nine and who, since a kid has derived his steadiness mostly from within himself, who has dialogued mostly with himself, I imagine that that will continue to describe my path. It seems to work all right.

Loneliness is a player that I believe intrudes on everyone's life, including mine. When I feel lonely and annoyed that my phone is quiet, I might call a friend to talk or make a date, or I might...just decide to decide that being lonely is OK...for awhile.

I'd be crazy to complain about my life.

978-0-595-38761-8
0-595-38761-6

Printed in the United Kingdom
by Lightning Source UK Ltd.
129887UK00001B/89/A